The untold story of broken treaties, black resistance, political fear and sacred ground.

America's Black Wall Street

by Chief Egunwale Amusan

Copyright ©2023
by Chief Egunwale Amusan

First Edition

Publisher
The Real Black Wall Street Tour LLC

For authors contact info and bio please visit:
www.realblackwallstreettour.com

ISBN 979-8-9892223-0-8 (bound) –
ISBN 979-8-9892223-1-5 (paperback) –
ISBN 979-8-9892223-2-2 (e-book)

All rights reserved. No part of this book may be reproduced in any form without permission of the Author.

Designed, typeset, and printed in America.

I dedicate this book to my children.
Like the sacred palm tree.
May your roots forever run deep

Table of Contents

8   Prologue

16   *Chapter One*
         The Real Black Wall Street

36   *Chapter Two*
         The Resistance: King Blue

58   *Chapter Three*
         Black Votes, White Rage

90   *Chapter Four*
         Testifying to Atrocity

118   Epilogue

124   Acknowledgments

130   Bibliography

Prologue

> *"I owe [telling the story] to the brave fellows who fought and died for a great cause on May 31 and June 1st and to the Race."*
>
> — A.J. Smitherman, Christmas 1921

    Whenever I go to Oaklawn Cemetery in Tulsa, Oklahoma, I pour libations in honor of those buried in mass graves, while praying in the native Yoruba tongue "Sun re o!" It means "rest in peace." In my community, I am called "Chief" because I am a trained and initiated Chief in the society of African Ancestral Wisdom. This is the wisdom of spiritual continuity and ancestral veneration. My title is *Alaagba*, which in context means elder custodian of those who have passed on. I feel a special stewardship for those who lie in unmarked graves and in mass burial sites like Oaklawn and other places in Tulsa.

    An untold number of these souls were victims of the Tulsa Race Massacre of 1921, and they cry out for justice. This includes the necessity for historical justice. To safeguard our interests, what began as a statement of resistance has been transformed into a legitimate business — The Real Black Wall Street Tour Company. As owner of The Real Black Wall Street Tour, I am committed to the notion that it is essential for us to tell our own stories with audacity, authenticity, and unwavering conviction. The following text reflects my story.

Raymond Lee Beard was just a tender baby of approximately 7 months old when one of the most heinous racist attacks against black people in U.S. history erupted on the night of May 31st, 1921. At the time, he was in the care of his sister and brother, Mary and Matthew Beard, who were living at 524 N. Greenwood Avenue, where they operated a laundry service out of their residence. My grandfather Raymond was miraculously carried to Sapulpa where his older sister Lilliane and her husband raised him to adulthood after the passing of his mother. He later served in World War II, returned to Greenwood in the 1940s, and lived there until his death in 2003.

After the massacre, my great uncle Matthew left Tulsa with his family and moved to Los Angeles, California. The fifth born child of Matthew and his wife Johnnie Mae, was named Matthew, Jr. He became known as the famed Little Rascals star Stymie Beard. According to census records, it appears that Matthew and his wife changed their names when they moved to Los Angeles after the massacre. I am not completely sure what happened to my grandfather's sister Mary after the Massacre. I've worked for many years to recover the real history of Greenwood and that of my family. I have been haunted by the fear that Mary was killed, and her body dumped in a mass grave like the one discovered at Oaklawn. Oral histories from survivors of the Massacre recount the abuse visited upon our dead during and after the Massacre.

Burned corpses were left exposed in the streets. Trucks were commandeered to carry bodies away to be dumped in unmarked graves, into the Arkansas River, or otherwise disposed of. Only eighteen bodies were buried with death certificates.[1] The rest "disappeared." These oral histories also record the agony of the people incarcerated at the Convention Hall, the ballpark, and the Tulsa Fairgrounds — people who were not permitted to recover or even search for the bodies of their loved ones. All this compounded violence feeds the ongoing trauma for the survivors and descendants of the Tulsa Race Massacre. Yet, the history of racism, slavery, and colonialism in and around Tulsa is not well known in America.

---

1 "No Graves Dug, Bodies of 18 Negroes Held," Tulsa Tribune (OK), June 2, 1921, 4.

1.1 *Photo Courtesy of Chief Amusan (Mary L. Beard seated left)*

I have come to think of the entire city as a mass grave. Oral histories from both white and black locals indicate the presence of possible mass graves throughout the town. One is Newblock Park, named after Klansman and former Mayor Herman F. Newblock. It is located to

11

the west of downtown. To the south is the site formerly known as Booker T. Washington Cemetery, now called Rolling Oaks. The Tulsa Fairgrounds between 21st and Yale is near another possible site. Oaklawn Cemetery is midtown's most documented mass grave site. Any ground holding Massacre victims becomes sacred. The ground holds our bones, our ashes, and our memories. The ground is also the basis for our future.

Denial, deflection, and deception about responsibility for the Tulsa Race Massacre on the part of white authorities continue to this day, despite the growing number of well-researched books and documentary films that demonstrate culpability. This book describes my journey to recover my own and my community's history in Greenwood. It adds to the knowledge about Greenwood, sometimes called "Black Wall Street," and contributes to the case for reparations. This book has more to say about politics—parties, registration, and voting—than most other works that have been published to date. My work as a history recovery specialist is personal as well as political. Readers of this book will learn about the many ways in which the history of Black Oklahomans as settlers, and Freedmen as modern citizens has been minimized, marginalized, or just plain ignored. These histories involve my own family members.

This book is not intended as a manifesto, exposé, or legal brief. It is not a polemic, or sermon. These pages "speak a radical truth about racism at the intersection of my personal story and historical narratives. Radical truth is sparked when people connect across differences. That spark carries the shimmer of empathy, the flash of understanding, and the glow of justice. The light itself is not a destination, but rather a method in the tradition of the writer bell hooks: "education as the practice of freedom." [2]

Today, many white Oklahomans tend to think that the Massacre has nothing to do with them. "This generation of Tulsans did not carry out a crime," asserts the current mayor, G.T. Bynum. Regarding reparations, he stated: "I don't think this generation of Tulsans should be financially penalized for something that criminals did 100 years ago." [3] This overlooks the fact that the City of Tulsa's police department was at the center of the Massacre. It could not have happened without the connivance and leadership of the men who controlled the city government and its police. The City of Tulsa *was* the criminal!

---

[2] bell hooks, *Teaching to Transgress: Education as the Practice of Freedom* (New York: Routledge, 1994).

[3] G.T. Bynum quoted in interview in Vice News Tonight, "Why the Tulsa Race Massacre is so Important to the Reparations Debate," (4 June 2021). https://www.youtube.com/watch?v=a4FcpT52hKs.

Meanwhile, white Tulsans continue to benefit from the historic dispossession and murder of Black and Native people, of which the Massacre forms only a dramatic part.

When I looked into the eyes of my grandfather or into the eyes of the still living survivors today, their message to me is clear: "Chief, don't let them forget us." In their words, I hear fear—the fear of being buried alive. Their words are also a call to action, and an invocation to the soil where memories are contained.

I want to give those Massacre victims interred at Oaklawn Cemetery a proper burial in a suitable place. I personally would love to move their remains to Standpipe Hill. Standpipe Hill was a place during the Massacre where Black people sought shelter. It is also a site where they took a stand to defend themselves. Some of these individuals were military veterans who had fought to defend the U.S. against foreign tyranny during World War I. They had been sworn to defend the U.S. Constitution, with all its promises of freedom. I'd like to turn the entire hill into a memorial that represents the spiritual reconciliation that Tulsa lacks. Many people, including myself, wish to honor the legacy of all the men and women who battled for Greenwood, bled in Greenwood, lived in Greenwood, built in Greenwood, and realized their vision and ambition in Greenwood. As Black journalist A.J. Smitherman put it in his epic poem "The Tulsa Riot and

Massacre," those who stood their ground on Standpipe Hill were "true martyrs for a sacred cause!" We must do this work to honor our ancestors. It is our duty to safeguard the sacred ground that our blood has consecrated.

CHAPTER ONE

The Real Black Wall Street

"Until the lion tells his side of the story, the tale of the hunt will always glorify the hunter."

— African Proverb

In 1985, I was a senior at Booker T. Washington High School in Tulsa, Oklahoma. In my memory, I can still see my younger self talking with my classmates about what we were going to do after we received our diplomas. Many of us were not interested in remaining in the state. Given the state of school textbooks at that time, it is no wonder that I used to joke with my best friend that riding in rodeos was Black Oklahomans' most significant achievement. We dreamed about moving to big cities like Atlanta, Dallas, or Houston. When I got to visit Atlanta, I was dazzled by the Black entrepreneurship on display in that city. I saw eye-opening models of Black success like cooperative economics and communal ownership that centered on the empowerment of communities. I felt inspired. I couldn't wait to return to Oklahoma to share what I learned with everyone.

When I returned to Tulsa, I believed that anything was possible. In 1995-96, the 75-year anniversary of the Tulsa Race Massacre stirred up a lot of emotion in our community. State Representative Don Ross and many others in Greenwood had worked hard to bring attention and resources to the Massacre. The next year, in 1997, I had a life-altering experience. I went to meet a close brother and friend named Changa in what was known as Deep Greenwood to visit the Future Vision Fine Arts Gallery, owned by Marsha Faida Campbell. That afternoon, we were fortunate enough to meet the author, Ron Wallace. Ron had published a book in 1992 titled *Black Wall Street: The Most Prolific African American Community in the History of America*. Talking to Ron and reading his book exposed me to an incredible legacy that I had not learned about in school. Ron had put together names, stories, and riveting details that revealed a Greenwood that I never knew existed. In 1921, Greenwood was already a prosperous, bustling, culturally rich, and politically rich district. The discovery of the Tulsa Massacre was a significant revelation, to say the least. In order to fully grasp the extent of the destruction it wrought, however, it is imperative that we attempt to imagine the unimaginable. The extent to which we may comprehend the significance of Greenwood lies in its status as a self-sufficient urban center encompassed by a complex web of more than fifty Black Oklahoma townships.[1] Nowhere in the United States has this phenomenon or network been successfully produced or reproduced. Biased textbooks written in a climate of white triumphalism had denied me access to this excellent legacy.[2] But that day was the turning point in my life. Now I was able to begin piecing together Black Wall Street, the Massacre and the Greenwood in which I was raised.

Recovering the positive history of Greenwood became the new center of my life. I developed relationships with some of the most influential people in the city. Some were survivors of the Tulsa Race Massacre, like Wess Young, Reverend Otis G. Clark, and Dr. Olivia Hooker. Eddie Faye Gates was a local high school teacher who did

---

[1] Larry O'Dell, "All-Black Towns," *The Encyclopedia of Oklahoma History and Culture*, https://www.okhistory.org/publications/enc/entry?entry=AL009.

[2] A textbook from the time describes Greenwood's prosperity in four sentences. It describes the "Tulsa Race Riot" in five paragraphs. The last sentence about the Massacre morally flattens the perpetrators and victims as follows: "The...nameless [black] roustabouts, oil millionaires, tired housewives, a famous newspaperwoman, even Tulsa's white rioters—their lives were the stuff of which history was made, full of events to be preserved and remembered forever." W. David Baird and Danney Goble, *The Story of Oklahoma* (Norman: University of Oklahoma Press, 1994), 384-386.

interviews with survivors and published a pathbreaking book, *Riot on Greenwood: The Total Destruction of Black Wall Street*, in 2003. Many people who cared about racial justice and Black history have shared their time, ideas, and research with me. These people include Billy Williams, Wess and Catherine Young, George Monroe, Ed Goodwin, Jim Goodwin, James Homer Johnson, Dorothy Dewitty, Dr. Vivian Clark-Adams, Regina Goodwin, Lee Roy Chapman, Attorney Damario Solomon Simmons, Randy Hopkins, Professor Charles Ogletree, Attorney Johnnie Cochran, and Attorney Adjoa Aiyetoro. These names are just a few of many.

As I learned about Black Tulsa and the great things Greenwood's pioneers did, my sense of Tulsa changed. I had renewed pride and appreciation for the legacy of Black cowboys, historic rodeos, and the Black towns that produced them. I learned so many things. I discovered the story of Marshal Bass Reeves (1838-1910), a former slave from Arkansas who was the first Black U.S. Federal Marshal to serve west of the Mississippi River. Appointed in the 1870s, Reeves served for thirty years in the Oklahoma area, arresting over 3,000 people and shooting some fourteen outlaws along the way. It is believed that Reeves was the inspiration for the character called *The Lone Ranger*, who debuted on a Chicago radio show in the 1930s.³ I experienced a strong sense of motivation to not only acquire knowledge, but also to disseminate and reshape the prevailing understanding of America's Black Wall Street in Tulsa. This demanded an overhaul of my preexisting knowledge of the history of Oklahoma, including the experiences of individuals from diverse cultural backgrounds, namely Black, white, and Native populations.

I found myself in many conversations about Greenwood. These touched on how stories about the Massacre were circulating in the media and in the publishing world. Tim Madigan's book *The Burning: Massacre, Destruction and the Tulsa Race Riot* came out in 2001. Others followed.⁴ Following the works of Ron Wallace and Eddie Faye Gates in the 1990s, many of the authors who were writing books about Greenwood or the Massacre were either not from here or the story wasn't connected to their own experiences. I am the type of person who requires a receipt. I appreciate irrefutable evidence. If you tell me

---

3 Arthur T. Burton, *Black Gun, Silver Star: The Life and Legend of Frontier Marshal Bass Reeves* (Lincoln: University of Nebraska Press, 2022).

4 James S. Hirsch, *Riot and Remembrance: The Tulsa Race War and its Legacy* (Boston: Houghton Mifflin Company, 2002). Alfred L. Brophy, *Reconstructing the Dreamland: The Tulsa Riot of 1921: Race, Reparations, and Reconciliation* (New York: Oxford University Press, 2003).

something, I require a receipt because I wish to avoid clapbacks. This is my personal motto.

A few years before the Centennial of the Massacre, I started to notice how the propaganda machine in Tulsa was gearing up to design a historic narrative that would cosmetically promote the image of Tulsa in the name of tourism. My relative and activist Kristi Williams is descended from Creek Freedmen. As she and I reconnected, we shared a concern that The City of Tulsa and various business interests would leverage for private gain the many activities, including neighborhood tours, planned for the Tulsa Race Massacre's Centennial Commemoration in 2021. We wanted to ensure that the history of Greenwood would be told through the lens of Massacre descendants and from the perspective of ongoing harm caused by the Massacre. We also wanted to engage in dialogue about racial trauma and the disruption of intergenerational wealth to help reframe the legacies of 1921 around the unmet need for justice in the here and now.

We felt compelled to unearth the truth in order to tell our own stories, from our own vantage point, through our own lens. I've spent many years talking about, reading about, and thinking about Black history and racism in Oklahoma and the United States. In grappling with the painful and troubling truths of racial injustice, I have concluded that true empathy with another person is impossible unless you know what's been taken from them, what's been lost, and what's been stolen. It is easy to dismiss and even redefine a collective traumatic experience if observed from a place of ignorance.

Try this experiment of imagination:

> *It's dawn. You're in bed or just stirring. The blast of a loud steam whistle invades your world. Running to the window, you see carloads of armed men unloading all around. Gunfire in the distance. As the whistle is replaced by a harsh buzzing sound that seems to be right over your head. Your very room starts to shake. At the door, your heart stands still. There is a great shadow in the sky. A cloud caused by fast approaching airplanes, flying low and in formation. More gunfire, faster now. Homes are ablaze! Neighbors, young and old, men, women, children, even babies in arms are on the road of flight. But to where? Hundreds of men, deputized by official authority, swarm from every direction. Mercenaries, murderers, and arsonists! Many in uniform. You are evicted. At gunpoint, you are dragged away to a camp. Glancing back, you see your home being looted of its fineries and family heirlooms like the spoils of war. Smoke begins to billow from a window. As you march, arms raised like a common criminal, you are immersed in the sights and sounds of a hell. The*

screams of those burned alive inside their homes for resisting or failing to surrender. The buzzing of the airplanes that never stops. Fire seems to fall from the sky itself. Bodies dragged through the streets. Degenerate rituals of violence. Wailing. Crying. Truckloads of bodies discarded in rivers, coal mines, and mass graves scattered all around. Like a curse, the lingering odor of burning and decaying flesh imprints itself like invisible ink on the pages of history. Your history.[5]

If one were to consider the historical experience of oneself or one's community, would it be a straightforward task to just relinquish any emotional attachment to it?

The primary objective of the Real Black Wall Street Tour is to provide individuals with a platform for engaging in open discourse and a comprehensive exploration of historical events. It is crucial to comprehend the significance of the devastation that occurred in Greenwood. It is equally imperative to avoid overlooking or minimizing the foundational excellence that contributed to the magnificent establishment of Greenwood in the first place.

---

[5] This short synopsis of the Massacre owes much to the eyewitness testimony presented by Mary E. Jones Parrish in *Race Riot 1921: Events of the Tulsa Disaster* (rev.ed), (Tulsa, OK: Out on a Limb Publishing, 1998).

This is how The Black Wall Street Tour began. We included the word "Real" in our company name because we wanted to deliver an experience that was organic, unedited, and unapologetic.

A trip to Jamaica in 2015 provided me with significant motivation and inspiration for composing this book. Myself and members of the African Ancestral Society traveled to Woodside Jamaica, where there is a cultural center called Blackspace. People from all around the world convene in this place to examine the legacy of slavery and what true emancipation can mean in the present. I had the distinct pleasure of meeting Jamaican Ethnographer, award winning novelist, and anthropologist Erna Brodber. Erna spearheads this powerful meeting of the minds. During the time of my visit, there were members of the academic community, artists, spiritualists, and grassroots communities present. During one of the sessions, the elder teacher, Yeye Amina Blackwood Meeks, said to us, "Head come before book." And I thought: "Wow! She just said a mouthful." Head come before book! Her words served as a reminder that stories in books begin in the mind. The actual storyteller is the head. Historians produce texts filled with regurgitated concepts from the mind. I thought to myself, I want to tell the Greenwood story from a deeper perspective than reciting what others have *said* or *read* about it. I wanted to tell it through the lens of those who *experienced* it. I started telling the story through the lens of those who *survived* it.

As a small child, my head start graduation ceremony was held in the basement of Vernon A.M.E. Church, a historic Black church in Tulsa that predated Oklahoma statehood. I know what it is like to be in Greenwood: to smell the air, to smell the earth, to stand where people in the past stood, to see the train tracks that are still there, and to smell the toxins from the old factories. You can also smell food nearby from the restaurants. You get a taste of everything. On the Real Black Wall Street Tour, I wanted people to have an experience that could not be gotten from a book. Or an experience that would make them ask, "Why *didn't* I get this from a book?" As I walk the streets of Greenwood and appreciate its people, it becomes clear that there is so much more to this story that is still unwritten. There is so much involved in really understanding a phenomenal place such as Greenwood. Even the Tour can't do it complete justice. I don't even like to use the term Black Wall Street, honestly, because the word "street" makes people think "linear" or "directional." We are not talking about a street, we are talking about an entire city within a city. That's what the "Real" in The Real Black Wall Street Tour represents. This time the Lion is telling its side of the story.

Student stories are among my favorites from the Tour. One of the earliest tours we conducted was with a group of 140 high school students from McLain High

School of Science and Technology in Tulsa. It was a beautiful thing. We started by collaborating with Dr. Tiffany Crutcher, who founded the Tulsa Community Remembrance Coalition, of which I am a member. We worked with Bryan Stevenson and the work being done in Montgomery, Alabama, as well as the National Memorial for Peace and Justice, which honors victims of lynching in the United States. We told the students that before we start the tour, we are going to have a ceremony. We planned for them to go to the area where a man named Henry Walker was lynched with lynching defined as the Memorial does—any act of violence or terror against a Black person committed between 1860 and 1940.

The ceremony involves collecting soil from a lynching site and creating a ritual to honor the person who was so cruelly murdered. The person's ashes and dust are in the earth, and they were denied a proper burial. By depriving the family of their loved one's body and denying the victim a dignified burial, the violence of lynching is compounded many times over. A rupture is created that demands healing. By collecting and reburying the soil in a special location, some of this rupture is knit back together.

On the occasion, we performed a soil collection for Mr. Walker. Very little is known about Henry Walker and many others who were killed in the Massacre; however, a proper burial is a sacred right. We collected

1.1 *McLain High School Students.*
Photo courtesy of Joseph Rushmore.

the soil on the grounds of Vernon A.M.E. Church, and all the students participated. I encouraged the students to call Mr. Walker's name, as is done in African and Indigenous traditions. There is a traditional saying about keeping people close—"Our ancestors do not die until we stop calling their names." As I spoke, the students were leaning on each other. Some of them were crying. It was cold out, and everyone was kind of huddled up. At that moment, I realized the impact of personalizing the story. We had students across all racial divides. They were all sharing this space together, seeing each other through a deeply human lens. By acknowledging a wrongful death and doing something meaningful to dignify the life lost, the students connected in a powerful way. I immediately asked myself how I could expand and build on this kind of experience.

When you walk down Greenwood Avenue, there are plaques on the ground that indicate where certain businesses were located before the district was destroyed. We took the students to the different sites, and we explained who owned this business or that building. We bring large historical photographs so they can see what it was like for people who lived during that time. We also brought the "after" photographs, to show what happened to these same people after the Massacre up to the point of urban renewal. We also provided a very full, holistic understanding of Greenwood and what it represented for Black people both in Oklahoma and across the United States. We teach that Greenwood was not merely a by-product of capitalism. Greenwood was a cultural product of cooperative economics and collective responsibility. An attitude that did not originate with the conditions of Jim Crow laws that supposedly forced blacks to spend money with one another.

I had some of the McLain students become figures in the story. I called out the names of people who lived in Greenwood: "I need someone to act as Jaunita Hooker," a survivor of the Tulsa Massacre. The girl who volunteered fit the bill; she was of Mexican, and African American descent. A Black student volunteered to play her husband, Samuel Hooker. The students were so excited! They got to act out history in a way that made them feel personally connected to the story. The idea of the Real Black Wall Street Tour is to bring historical information and book learning to life. I now call it the Public Classroom. Together, we reclaimed the history that had been omitted from their own history books. We gave them ownership.

The tour confronts people with the fact that the Massacre was not perpetrated by a "mob" that acted spontaneously, but by white citizens who were deputized by governmental law enforcement to imprison and murder

1.2 *Student member of the Trio Program at Southern University of Shreveport Louisiana. The Trio Program consists of three programs: Upward Bound, Talent Search, and Student Support. Photo courtesy of author.*

Black people and who were given weapons to loot, burn, and bomb the Greenwood neighborhood. This confrontation is one of the most dramatic parts of the Tour. People get to absorb the enchantment of what Greenwood was, as well as the outrage that this could happen to American citizens on domestic soil. The Tour places people in that powerful, important, and unpleasant zone that I refer to as "the balance."

I have led scores, possibly hundreds, of Real Black Wall Street Tours in Greenwood. Students and school groups make up a large portion of the visitors. Families and descendants add so much value to the work we do. Many of the families who tour have relatives connected to Greenwood. Walking the streets and taking in all the sights, stories, and atmosphere brings them closer to the memories of loved ones. One of the things that makes this tour so compelling is the fact that it is in no way a cookie cutter experience. People are pleased to discover that the tour is not a lecture. It is a dialogue. People bring their own questions and curiosity. Many groups have come to us asking for the truth once they realize the narratives presented in school or the media do not add up. They ask, "Why does no one seem to know what happened to Sarah Page or Dick Rowland beyond urban legend?" "Was the massacre preplanned?" "Where did the planes come from that bombed Greenwood?" "Was the Massacre really the product of white jealousy and greed?"

I know a human connection has been made when the tour turns into a partnership. A great example is the young professionals who are members of the Jewish Federation of Tulsa. This mention is important because the Tulsa Race Massacre resonates with the Christian pogroms carried out against Jews in Europe for centuries. The Holocaust, ethnic cleansing, and genocide all echo in the horrors perpetrated against the people of Greenwood. Jews in Oklahoma historically endured cross burnings and other forms of intimidation by the Ku Klux Klan. In 2021, I wrote an article for the *Tulsa Jewish Review* about the Real Black Wall Street Tour.[6]

I have given Tours for notable people, like the award-winning actor Tom Hanks who visited Tulsa to promote his new novel *The Making of Another Major Motion Picture Masterpiece*. He took time to express the deep impact of the Tour before a sold out audience at the Tulsa Performing Arts Center. Hanks also wrote an opinion piece for the *New York Times* called "You should learn about the Tulsa Race Massacre." In a Youtube video, he declared how "angry" he was that the Tulsa story had been left out of his education, stating that such an

---

6 Chief Egunwale Amusan, "The Real Black Wall Street Tour" (p. 11) and Phil Goldfarb, "Jews and the Tulsa Race Massacre," (pp. 12-13) in the *Tulsa Jewish Review* (May 2021). https://www.jewishtulsa.org/wp-content/uploads/2021/05/21-05-TJR_May_Web.pdf

"editorial decision" was wrong and that it did "a disservice to all of American history."[7]

I have toured students from educational institutions like MIT, Oklahoma University, and Southern University at Shreveport, as well as many of the US Military Branches. We have also toured college and professional athletes, including the NFL and the MLS. We were the first to tour our local Pro Soccer team, FC Tulsa, which has players from around the globe.

Elected officials also come through. We had two presidential candidates visit Greenwood in 2020, Beto O'Rourke and Cory Booker. Beto is from Texas and made connections with the legacy of the Ku Klux Klan in both states, which share a border. Cory Booker is a U.S. Senator from New Jersey. Oklahoma was a little bit of unknown territory for him, but he connected with the stories, the people, and the place, which is Greenwood. At a gathering at Vernon A.M.E. Church after the tour, he stated the following about Greenwood and its history:

"Our nation's history is a history of wretchedness and pain. We don't tell the truth of our history enough. It weakens our very being when we don't tell the truth

---

7 Tom Hanks, "Opinion: You Should Learn about the Tulsa Race Massacre," *New York Times* (4 June 2021). For video see: https://www.youtube.com/watch?v=lKgSX5KI1Iw

1.3 FC Tulsa on *The Real Black Wall Street Tour.*
Photo courtesy of Victor Schwanke

of our history because the greatness of this country isn't that we have been bereft of violence and torture and terrorism on our own soil. The greatness of our nation lies in how we overcame that. How every generation did not give up. They kept fighting. They kept working. They kept struggling. They kept moving forward despite unimaginable pain. I felt that pain when I touched the scarred and charred bricks of a great community here in Greenwood. A community that thrived. Where Black journalists and Black educators and Black businesspeople formed a thriving American town that was a light of promise--and then it was torched and burned. We are here because of folks who never gave up on the dream of America." [8]

---

8 "Cory Booker Visits Black Wall Street." https://www.youtube.com/watch?v=kwJSMdoD8uQ viewed 6-25-3023.

33

Sometimes we get surprise visitors on the Tour. One surprise visitor became a partnership that landed me in *Variety* magazine, which covers the motion picture industry. In 2021, filmmakers Salima Korama and Patrick Altema came to Greenwood to create a documentary. The result was "Dreamland: The Burning of Black Wall Street," a CNN film produced by LeBron James. The film won two Emmy awards, one for outstanding graphic design and one for art direction. This project was about uplifting the stories of the survivors and descendants of the Tulsa Race Massacre. I am proud that the story has been told in the gripping and accessible medium of film, that will last for generations. The everyday storytelling on the ground in Greenwood continues.

The Real Black Wall Street Tour is an institution created to make the classroom public in a world where critical race theory prohibitions continue to reinforce anti-Black sentiments. The 2021 passage of Oklahoma House Bill 1775 made it illegal to teach Oklahoma students that "one race or sex is inherently superior to another race or sex" or that "an individual, by virtue of his or her race or sex, is inherently racist, sexist, or oppressive, whether consciously or unconsciously."[9] This creates an easy ex-

---

9 https://sde.ok.gov/sites/default/files/documents/files/HB%20 1775%20Emergency%20Rules.pdf

cuse to send the study of history, including its horrors, to the back of the academic bus. Hear no evil, speak no evil, see no evil...and now, study no evil.

Making apologies, restoring the damage, and admitting responsibility for the Massacre's devastation, including the long-term impacts, are all part of historic justice. It is not about shame or guilt. It is a matter of accountability. It is vital that we spread the stories through all accessible channels. Greenwood's legacy may be the greatest hidden story in American history.

CHAPTER TWO

The Resistance: King Blue

> *"Thus, in the underground of our unwritten history much of that which is ignored defies our inattention by continuing to grow and have consequences."*
>
> —*Ralph Ellison*[1]

Building The Real Black Wall Street Tour meant uncovering the stories that were ignored in mainstream media and history textbooks. Learning the truth about Black Wall Street and the Greenwood neighborhood was also a crash course in the "politics of history." It is a cliche that the winners write history. The wealthy and the powerful have long had the resources to publicize their version of events and to give themselves credit through monuments, statues, and named buildings. This idea of self-interested

---

1 Ralph Ellison, Going to the Territory, (New York: Vintage, 1986), 126.

history is an old one. It was stated in cynical terms by French Enlightenment thinkers like Voltaire and popularized by Napoleon: "History is a set of lies agreed upon." But one of Oklahoma's most significant Black figures, the genius Ralph Ellison, took a less jaded and more humane view of the politics of history. He warned that despite what people ignore or deny, the truths of history continue to "grow and have consequences" in our lives and in society. Truths do not disappear; lies do not stay quiet. They haunt our dreams, prick our imaginations, and peck at our conscience. They show up in our behaviors, our politics, our art, and our neighborhoods. That is certainly my experience as an Oklahoman.

I can remember sitting in class at George Washington Carver Middle School in Tulsa and listening intently as my teacher told us about Native American history as it relates to Oklahoma. In the 1830s, the U.S. Government forcibly relocated the Cherokee, Chickasaw, Choctaw, Creek, and Seminole tribes from their historic homelands in the southeastern United States. The U.S. government established Indian Territory in modern-day eastern Oklahoma as a separate area of land where the tribes had to live in accordance with the Indian Removal Act. This law was passed so that white settlers in Georgia, the Carolinas, Florida, and elsewhere could secure Indian lands for themselves. About 60,000 tribal members were cleared from their homelands. The wealthy among them traveled west in their own wagons and were able to make some choices about when to leave. But a great number made a forced march on foot in the winter of 1838 during which many people lost their lives. This deadly march is known as the Trail of Tears, memorializing the painful exile and economic dispossession of Native people.[2] I recall the overwhelming sorrow I felt as a young student when I learned that another group of people in the U.S. suffered similarly to Black Americans.

Oklahoma itself was created in 1907 by fusing Indian Territory and Oklahoma Territory. Outside the statehood museum in Guthrie stands a statue of Mr. Cowboy and Miss Indian, memorializing Oklahoma statehood as a happily married couple. What this statue and my teacher's classroom lesson did not tell me was that all five of the Native American groups that endured removal, sometimes referred to as the Five Civilized Tribes, owned slaves. Historians estimate that several thousand individuals on the Trail of Tears were enslaved people of African descent. Many Tribes also purchased more slaves when they arrived in Indian Territory to work the land, and it is noteworthy that all of these tribes provided support to

---

2 Amy H. Sturgis, *The Trail of Tears and Indian Removal*, (Westport, Conn: Greenwood Press, 2007). Grant Foreman, *Indian Removal: The Emigration of the Five Civilized Tribes of Indians*, (Norman: University of Oklahoma Press, 1986).

the Confederacy during the Civil War.[3]

I did not get the whole story in school. Oklahoma history is told, like so much of American history, as having two sides and only two sides — White and Native.

The 13th Amendment to the Constitution of 1865 prohibited slavery or involuntary servitude within the United States. After the Civil War, the federal government ordered slavery to end in Indian Territory. A treaty was signed in 1866 codifying these new terms with the Five Civilized Tribes, but each Nation navigated its own politics of race and citizenship. These politics played out for decades and were not resolved until the Dawes Act broke up tribal lands around 1900. In the meantime, thousands of African-descended former slaves, referred to as Freedmen, lived in political limbo.[4]

I only learned about this history through my own family. I am descended from Choctaw Freedmen. My wife is descended from Chickasaw Freedmen.[5] Most Okla-

---

3 Amanda L. Paige, Fuller L. Bumpers, and Daniel F. Littlefield, Jr., *Chickasaw Removal* (Ada, Okla: Chickasaw Press, 2010). Bradley R. Clampitt, *The Civil War and Reconstruction in Indian Territory* (Lincoln: University of Nebraska Press, 2015).

4 Daniel F. Littlefield, *The Chickasaw Freedmen: A People without a Country* (Westport, Conn: Greenwood Press, 1980).

5 On my family story and the Choctaw freedmen, see National Geographic's "2892 Tulsa" project. https://storymaps.arcgis.com/collections/be2f71b037114de9a298e3387a62a78e?item=1. See also Caleb Gayle, *We Refuse to Forget: A True Story of Black Creeks, American Identity, and Power* (New York: Riverhead Books, 2022).

homa histories omit the history, hardships, and accomplishments of these African-descended people, families, and communities. Similarly, little attention is accorded to all-Black communities such as Boley, Tallahassee, and Langston, as well as some 48 others founded around the turn of the century by African-American settlers from neighboring states.

The story of Edwin McCabe and his idea for an all-Black state in Oklahoma is another little-known feature of this history.[6] Exposure of this hidden history is mostly thanks to the efforts of Black Oklahomans who have done the research, memorialization, and education themselves.[7] Yet the story of the Freedmen of the Five Civilized Tribes in Indian Territory remains one of the least known parts of Oklahoma and U.S. history.[8]

The story of my children's fourth great-grandfather, King Blue, is emblematic of the negative stereotyping and

---

6 "A Negro State," *The Appeal* [St. Paul, MN] (8 march 1890): 1& 2. James N. Leiker, "African Americans and Boosterism," *Journal of the West* 42, no. 4 (Fall 2003): 25–34; Nell Irvin Painter, *Exodusters: Black Migration to Kansas after Reconstruction* (New York: Knopf, 1977).

7 The classic text is Arthur Lincoln Tolson, The Black Oklahomans: A History. 1541-1972 (New Orleans: Edwards Print Company, 1974).

8 Oklahoma City Public Schools 9th Grade Curriculum: https://docs.google.com/document/d/13b-VtRjC7jCBCg91XzU3DKNSgxCnCSsn8ixtzRjPKQY/edit (viewed 6-20-2023).

devaluation of all the Freedmen in the Oklahoma story. The story also tells us something about the politics of writing and memorializing history in the United States. King Blue is part of the long history of slavery, Black resistance, and struggle in Oklahoma.

King Blue was part of a large family with roots in Mississippi. When his descendants enrolled as Chickasaw Freedmen in 1898 under the Dawes Allotment Act, his wife Mary was 76 years old and recently widowed. Benjamin Franklin Colbert, who arrived in Oklahoma from Desoto, Mississippi during the Indian Removal to Indian Territory, owned King Blue and 25 other enslaved people. Winchestor Colbert owned King Blues' wife until 1866. Winchestor was the Governor of the Chickasaw Nation for several terms.[9] The Colberts were a prominent and powerful Chickasaw family descended from a white Scotch trader who intermarried with Chickasaws. King Blue's owner Benjamin Franklin Colbert had a large cotton plantation in Bryan County near the Texas border.

---

9 Cards #135 (King Blue, son) and #78 (Mary Blue, wife), September, 1898. Applications for Enrollment in the Five Civilized Tribes, RG 75, National Archives and Records Administration [NARA] (viewed online 6-18-2023). See cards 67 (Sallie), 79 (Susie), 81 (Elsie), 91 (Peter), and 127 (George) for the other children of Mary and King, Sr. See also 12th Census of the United States, Indian Territory, Chickasaw Nation, Sheet 11 (B).

2.1 Enrollment Cards for the Five Civilized Tribes, 1898-1914; NAI Number: 251747

Starting in 1853, Colbert ran a lucrative ferry service on the Red River. Today, the site of his ferry is on the National Register of Historic Places, and the nearby town of Colbert bears his name. Ironically, it became the seat of Blue County.[10]

I honor King Blue as an advocate for Freedmen's citizenship rights and a fighter for land justice. Unlike the Colberts, the Blue family is hard to find in the archive or on a map. King Blue's story enters the historical record in fragments.

---

10 Larry O'Dell, "Colbert's Ferry," *The Encyclopedia of Oklahoma History and Culture*, https://www.okhistory.org/publications/enc/entry?entry=CO018.

His name is on a document from 1882 entitled "Memorial of the Chickasaw Freedmen." In this petition, King Blue and three others, Isaac Alexander, Fletcher Frazier, and John Dyer, requested that the U.S. Government honor the Choctaw-Chickasaw treaty of 1866. The treaty's terms freed the enslaved population of the Tribes, established their rights as full U.S. citizens, and covered the expenses for those who wished to migrate out of Indian Territory. The Chickasaw actively supported the Confederacy, but the petitioners carefully pointed out that they themselves were "volunteer soldiers" on the side of the U.S. during the conflict and that "no one...took part in the war against the Union." For nearly 20 years, former slaves were treated neither as equals in the Chickasaw Nation nor as free citizens of the United States. "As things now exist so far as the persons of African descent in the nations are concerned, the word freedmen is a sham," complained the petitioners.[11]

The Chickasaw had not freed their slaves. Slaveholders were aggrieved to lose the valuable labor that had helped build the Chickasaw Nation. But if emancipation was the only option, then the Chickasaw leadership wanted no part of their former slaves. Rather than compel

---

[11] "Memorial of the Chickasaw Freedmen," http://www.african-nativeamerican.com/chickmem.htm.

```
                                    FREEDMAN

     Chickasaw Freedmen Card 78.
          In the matter of the application of Mary Blue for enrollment
     as a Chickasaw Freedman.
          Mary Blue being sworn by Commissioner A.S.McKennon says:
          I am about 76 years old. I have no husband. I was a slave and
     belonged to Winchester Colbert . I was freed as his slave.
                                       Stonewall, Sept. 2, '98
     Mary Blue
              enrolled.
```

2.2 *"Chickasaw Freedman Card 78" for Mary Blue, 1898.RG 75, National Archives of the United States*

the Chickasaws to adopt the Freedmen when it had the leverage, the U. S. Government gave the Nation a loophole. Due to their allegiance to the Confederacy, the Choctaws and Chickasaws were forced to pay reparations by ceding a large part of southeastern Oklahoma to the U. S. Calling it a payment for the land, $300,000 was to be held in trust for the tribes for two years. The two tribes got that money if they made their Freedmen full citizens. Once the two years passed without an adoption, however, the Chickasaw share of the trust, $75,000, transferred under the treaty to the benefit of Freedmen at the rate of $100 per head, but *only if they chose to remove themselves from the Nation!* The U. S. was supposed to handle the removal, using the forfeited funds. The U. S. and the Chickasaw Nation further agreed that those who remained (or returned after removing) were to have "no benefit" of the trust money. By refusing adoption, the Chickasaw Nation was able to wash its hands of the Freedmen for what it now calls a "nominal payment."[12]

In the end, few Freedmen wanted to abandon the home where many of them had been born. By the forfeiture of $75,000, the Chickasaw Nation was freed from all responsibility to the tribe's former "human property." Over the years, the Nation provided not even a crude wooden school for Freedmen children. The clever 1866 treaty was negotiated for the Chickasaw by another slave-owning Colbert. The U. S. Government appears to have pocketed the $75,000.[13]

With each passing year after 1866, the population of Chickasaw Freedmen grew. In 1873, the Chickasaw legislature passed an act purporting to adopt the Freedmen. It was sent to the U. S. Congress for approval, but nothing happened. The Chickasaw legislature quickly reversed course and began passing a series of acts demanding the removal of the Freedmen from Chickasaw land.

---

12 https://www.chickasaw.tv/events/treaty-of-1866

13 Littlefield, *The Chickasaw Freedmen*, 21-25, 39-40, 51-53, 63-67, 112-13, 140-158, 163, 187, 191-211, 218-227.

Meanwhile, the Black population was also augmented by migrants from other states with no connection to the Tribes. At first, the Chickasaw tried to re-enslave and even sell this migrant group, but eventually passed legislation requiring their removal in 1882. Federal funds were allocated to the Chickasaw for the Freedmen's removal that year as well.[14]

These moves likely prompted King Blue's 1882 petition to the Federal Government for real emancipation according to the 1866 treaty, as well as for the right to remain in the Territory. "For many and grave reasons we do not elect to remove," Blue and the Memorialists wrote. "As natives, we are attached to the localities of our birth and childhood."[15]

King Blue does not appear in the record again until the summer of 1894. He was probably living near Stonewall in Pontotoc County. News wires from Guthrie and

---

14 Littlefield, *The Chickasaw Freedmen*, chapter six. Parthena Louise James, "Reconstruction in the Chickasaw Nation, 1867-1877" (MA Thesis, Oklahoma State University, Stillwater, 1963), 33-57. Thomas F. Andrews, "Freedmen in Indian Territory: A Post-Civil War Dilemma," *The Journal of the West* 4, no. 3 (July 1965): 367-76.

15 "Memorial of the Chickasaw Freedmen." Celia E. Naylor-Ojurongbe, "'Born and Raised Among these People, I don't want to know any other': Slaves' Acculturation in Nineteenth-Century Indian Territory," in *Confounding the Color Line: The Indian-Black Experience in North America* ed. James Brooks (Lincoln: University of Nebraska Press, 2002), 161-191.

Wichita were picked up by newspapers as far away as New York City, San Francisco, and Idaho. These reports announced that King Blue, the "ruler of the Negro Indians" among the Chickasaw, was "on the warpath" in a "marauding tour" that was "terrorizing the whole country." Fired by "whiskey" in his "savage soul," this "desperado" was stirring up an "open rebellion."[16] No actual alleged reasons for raiding were given. Instead, Blue was turned into a racist object lesson — a "negro outlaw — useful for justifying the breakup of Tribal governments that so poorly regulated their own Nations.[17]

By contrast, Indian Agent and future U.S. Senator Robert L. Owen listed King Blue as one of the "leading men" in the community in these same years.[18] A small acknowledgment of King Blue's leadership slipped in between the lines in the newspapers. One report noted that "while an old man," King Blue was "very strong physically and a natural leader of surprising tact." The writer acknowledged that he "had been at the head of

---

16 "King Blue on the Warpath," *Caldwell [Idaho] Tribune* (19 September 1894): 4; "Negro Indians in Rebellion," *Leavenworth Times* (20 September 1894), 1; "King Blue's Raid," *Wichita Daily Eagle* (20 September 1894): 2. "Make the Indians Scratch" *Western Kansas World* (23 September 1894), 4.

17 Squib, *Wichita Daily Eagle* (21 September 1894), 4.

18 Littlefield, *The Chickasaw Freedmen*, 147.

the half-blood negroes in the Chickasaw nation since the [civil] war," indicating decades of community trust and leadership experience.[19]

The timing and nature of King Blue's 1894 "raid" deserves attention. On August 15th, 1894, the U. S. Congress finally approved the 1873 Chickasaw law adopting the Freedmen into the tribe. The Chickasaw would have none of it, arguing that the 1873 law was superseded by repeated legislative demands for Freedmen removal. The Dawes Commission report of November 20, 1894 concluded that:

"The Chickasaws denied that they had ever adopted the freedmen. They now treat the whole class as aliens without any legal right to abide among them, or to claim any protection under their laws. They are shut out of the schools of the tribe, and from their courts, and are granted no privileges of occupancy of any part of the land for a home, and are helplessly exposed to the hostilities of the citizen Indian and the personal animosity of the former master. Peaceable, law-abiding, and hard-working, they have sought in vain to be regarded as a part of the people to whose wealth their industry is daily contributing a very essential portion. They number in that (Choctaw) tribe about 4,000, while the Chickasaws number 3,500. The United States is bound by solemn treaty to place these

---

19 "The Chickasaw Nation," *New York Times* (12 July 1896), 32.

freedmen securely in the enjoyment of their rights as Chickasaw Indians, and can not with honor ignore the obligation."[20]

Considering this sentiment, there should have been no doubt as to why King Blue demanded that Congress intervene to assure full Chickasaw citizenship rights for himself and others who believed themselves to be free and entirely deserving. The failure of the tribal and U.S. governments to resolve the status issue forced free people of African descent to traverse a new trail of tears in Indian Territory, musing on an uncertain future. Since King Blue had made plain the community's preference for Chickasaw citizenship with all its advantages, anger at continued Chickasaw opposition is understandable. The raid transpired a few weeks after Chickasaw rejection of the ineffective Congressional act purporting to approve citizenship for the Freedmen.

What kind of "raid" was undertaken? Blue and his band focused on a very specific white man, Canadian born Dr. George H. Traux, who played an important role in both Pontotoc County and the Chickasaw Nation. Traux was the postmaster, so he was the public face of the U.S. Government in the area. In rural communities, the post office served as a meeting place, organizing cen-

---

20 S. Misc. Doc. No. 24, 53rd Cong., 3rd Sess. (1894), 11.

ter, and information hub; postmasters frequently resided at the post office. Despite the inflamed language in the media, no one was injured, much less killed in this raid. The potential exploitation of media exaggeration by the Chickasaw tribe could have been employed as a means to reinforce their advocacy for the expulsion of freedmen by the federal government, aligning with their preexisting acts. Traux and his wife were removed from their living quarters and bound in the yard. According to newspa-

> **IN OPEN REBELLION.**
>
> **A Chickasaw Negro-Indian Leader Is On the Warpath.**
>
> WICHITA, Kan., Sept. 19.—A special to the Eagle from Stonewall, Chickasaw nation, brings information to the effect that King Blue, leader of the Chickasaw negro-Indians, is in open rebellion. The insurrectionists have gone out on a marauding tour and are terrorizing Indian citizens and especially the squaw-men.

2.3 *"In Open Rebellion."*
Caldwell [Idaho] Tribune, 26 September 1894, p. 4

per reports, the band took food and drink and busted up some furniture before departing. This raid left a mark on property that, at least in part, symbolized the unreliable and unresponsive federal government.

George Traux also held practical and symbolic importance to Chickasaw Freedmen. He was a doctor who assisted in the health care of the community. King's relative, Minney Blue, was a midwife who worked side by side with Traux. In 1886, Traux married a Chickasaw woman, Mary C. Colbert, which made him a tribal member. The couple now represented the enslavers in the community.[21] The approval of Chickasaw adoption by the Federal Government may have been viewed as a great injury to the tribal nation since by 1893, the Black population outnumbered the Chickasaw. The tribe feared black political control over the nation. Yet, the freedmen remained a people without a country. [22] With generations of children growing up without fundamental rights, the lack of property ownership, political empowerment, and access to education was a particularly sensitive issue. George Traux might have once been seen as a friend of the Chickasaw Freedmen, but he was now seen as a traitor, especially considering speculations over a land dispute.

In 1896, two years after the raid, King Blue and his son Joe met with Chickasaw leadership and wrote letters

---

21 Card #38, Applications for Enrollment in the Five Civilized Tribes, RG 75, NARA (viewed online 6-18-2023)

22 Littlefield, *The Chickasaw Freedmen*, chapter 5. Ellen Cain, "'The Golden Days': Taylor and Mary Ealy, Citizenship, and the Freedmen of Chickasaw Indian Territory, 1874-77," *Chronicles of Oklahoma* 92, no. 1 (Spring 2014), 54-77

to the Secretary of Interior in Washington, D.C. for clarification of their status.[23] Blue was making another effort at diplomacy as enrollment and allotment under Dawes loomed. That same year, however, a negative press account took another swipe at "Old King Blue." A *New York Times* article with a byline of Tishomingo (the Chickasaw capital) claimed that Blue and his "gang of blackskins" were in "open rebellion" terrorizing white farmers, especially "squaw men" (white men married to Native women).[24]

Unlike the other so-called Five Civilized Tribes, the Chickasaw never adopted their Freedmen, denying them and their descendants a wide range of housing, education, medical care and other forms of support still provided by the Nation to its citizens.[25] The U. S. managed to require that Chickasaw Freedmen who successfully navigated the Dawes allocation process would receive land equal in value to an average 40 acres in the Choctaw and Chickasaw Nations. This contrasted to an outright 320 acres

---

23 Littlefield, *The Chickasaw Freedmen*, 169-70.

24 "The Chickasaw Nation," *New York Times* (12 July 1896), 32. This suspect report largely repeated details from the 1894 raid and seems planted by Chickasaw leadership (based in Tishomingo) in support of the old agenda of removing the Freedmen in exchange for emancipation, especially since allotment seemed imminent. The story was picked up by the *Maryville Times* [Tennessee] (13 August 1896), 3.

25 https://chickasaw.net/Services.aspx

per head for Chickasaw citizens.[26] The U. S. Government also reimbursed the Chickasaw Nation for the value of the Freedmen allocation. The allocations to the Freedmen cost the Choctaw and Chickasaw Nations nothing.[27]

Documentation of the enrollment for land allotments that began in the fall of 1898 notes that King Blue had died, but not how. Who knows if this hero, who had been slandered as a "tyrant" met an untimely, perhaps wrongful death? The Colbert family is remembered and memorialized with an historic marker near the ferry site on the Red River. But King Blue had his name dragged through the mud in the newspapers from coast to coast after his earnest efforts to protect and defend the rights of his family and his people. He will always be remembered as a King who fought to lead his people to a promised land.

In 2021, Juneteenth became a national holiday in the United States. The holiday commemorates the day that a union army officer, Gordon Grainger, rode into Galveston, Texas on June 19, 1865. He informed the still enslaved residents of the town that the Emancipation Proclamation had freed them more than two years earlier. The holiday is becoming well known. So is the incredible sto-

---

26 https://www.chickasaw.tv/events/allotment-act
27 Littlefield, *The Chickasaw Freedmen*, 198-203.

ry of Opal Lee, the retired schoolteacher from Tarrant County, Texas who walked — at age 89 — all the way to Washington D.C. to put the request for the holiday before President Joe Biden of the United States. She walked two-and-a half miles a day to symbolize the two-and-a-half years it took for enslaved people in Texas to learn that they were free.

Descendants of the Freedmen of Indian Territory, however, cannot authentically celebrate Juneteenth. Nor is Emancipation Day, January 1, (the date the Emancipation Proclamation was signed by Abraham Lincoln) a real holiday for us, though it was celebrated for several generations after slavery as a community holiday, mostly in Black churches. Our Freedmen story doesn't fit these patterns and is therefore easily overlooked. In fact, legal tussles between the Tribes and descendants of the Freedman continue. In 2017, the Cherokee sued Raymond Nash (et. al.) to resist the citizenship claim of these descendants of former slaves of the Nation. A U.S. district judge issued a memorandum opinion in favor of the defendants, finding that the "Cherokee Freedmen have a present right to citizenship in the Cherokee Nation that is coextensive with the rights of native Cherokees."[28]

---

28 *Cherokee Nation v. Nash*, 267 F. Supp. 3d 86 (D.D.C. 2017). https://casetext.com/case/cherokee-nation-v-nash-4

The Muskogee (Creek) Nation has also attempted to backtrack. In 1979, the tribal constitution was revised to remove anyone who is not a Creek "by blood." Attorney Damario Solomon-Simmons, founder of the research and advocacy foundation Justice for Greenwood, is leading a fight for citizenship for the Black Creeks. Solomon contends that neither the tribal constitution nor the constitution itself has the legal authority to revoke the 1866 treaty that granted former slaves and their descendants full citizenship and tribal rights. Stunningly, Solomon-Simmons' suit has just been crowned with a victory. On September 27, 2023, Muskogee Nation District Judge Denise Mouser defied her own Nation's attorney general by ruling that the 1866 treaty remains the "supreme law of the land" and guarantees that the Creek Freemen and their descendants, regardless of their "blood" status, shall "have and enjoy all the rights and privileges of native citizens of the Nation. The suit proves that hope is not lost and that resistance to being swept into the dustpan of history is not in vain.

What would it take to include the Freedmen of Indian Territory and their descendants when we invoke "Civil Rights" or "Freedom Fighters" in the tradition of Black history? How many children graduate from public high schools in this country without ever hearing of the Freedmen? Today, the Cherokee, Choctaw, Seminole, Chickasaw, and Creeks each have a Freedman subgroup within their Nations. Much work remains in Oklahoma and the United States to create cultural and political space for the history of the Freedmen.

"Self-trust is the essence of heroism. It is the state of the soul at war, and its ultimate objects are the last defiance of falsehood and wrong, and the power to bear all that can be inflicted by evil agents. It speaks the truth, and it is just, generous, hospitable, temperate, scornful of petty calculations, and scornful of being scorned. It persists; it is of an undaunted boldness, and of a fortitude not to be wearied out."

— Ralph Waldo Emerson

CHAPTER THREE

Black Votes and White Rage

*"The Republican party offers us little.
The Democratic party offers us nothing."*

—R.R. Church,[1]

Several well-researched books explain the causes of the Tulsa Race Massacre. Typically, these works have little to say about political parties or elections. They mostly argue that racist, corrupt law enforcement goaded by a racist, irresponsible media is at the toxic center of it all.[2] Yet these political elements are important grounding for my own view, and I will lay out some of these themes as context.

---

1 "Why I am for Hoover," Chicago (ILL) Defender (November 3, 1928), 3.

2 Oklahoma Commission to Study the Tulsa Race Riot of 1921, "Tulsa Race Riot: A Report by the Oklahoma Commission to Study the Tulsa Race Riot of 1921," (Oklahoma City, 2001). Copy in Oklahoma Historical Society.

Historical amnesia has caused us to forget that one of the greatest threats to the maintenance of white supremacy is Black political power and independence. This is not mere speculation or fantasy. These are historically documented facts that have demonstrated the consequences of race-based fear and panic, which has resulted in barbaric massacres, such as:

September 28th, 1868 — a two week long massacre in Opelousas, Louisiana. Just one year prior, Louisiana voters had ratified a state constitution that granted Black men the right to vote and gain access to public schools. In an effort to terrorize, intimidate, and suppress voter turnout, about 250 black people were massacred.[3]

Easter Sunday, April 13, 1873 — the Colfax Massacre in Grant Parish, Louisiana. A white mob of hundreds of armed white men killed and wounded close to two hundred black Americans who were defending the Parish courthouse from democratic seizure following the state's controversial 1872 gubernatorial election. This is very reminiscent of the black defenders in Tulsa who offered to help defend the courthouse on May 31st 1921.[4]

---

[3] "The Deadliest Massacre in Reconstruction-Era Louisiana Happened 150 Years Ago," https://www.smithsonianmag.com/history/story-deadliest-massacre-reconstruction-era-louisiana-180970420/

[4] "The 1872 Colfax Massaacre Set Back the Reconstruction Era," https://www.smithsonianmag.com/smart-news/1873-colfax-massacre-crippled-reconstruction-180958746/

November 10, 1898 — the Wilmington Massacre in North Carolina. Once again, a white mob committed hate crimes against the elected biracial body. This was a governmental coup that led to a violent massacre in which at least 60 were killed. On November 9th, the night before the overturned election, Democrat Alfred Waddell, the mob's leader, said, "We will no longer be ruled, and will never again be ruled by men of African origin."[5]

The exterminationist mentality unleashed in the atrocity in Tulsa was many decades in the making. It has deep roots in the racist scapegoating of Black people in the United States. Films like *Birth of a Nation* (1915) enshrined "the Negro" as a threat to the body politic. Fears about the integrity of the nation were projected onto the body of white women, imagined to be vulnerable to sexual assault by menacing Black men. *Birth of a Nation* valorized the lynching-for-rape drama on the big screen, celebrated the Ku Klux Klan members as heroes, and motivated the creation of the modern KKK at Stone Mountain, Georgia in 1916. Actual lynch mobs in the U.S. have ended the lives of nearly 4,000 people.[6] Oklahoma's

---

5 "Lost History of an American Coup D'Etat," https://www.theatlantic.com/politics/archive/2017/08/wilmington-massacre/536457/

6 W. Fitzhugh Brundage, ed., *Under Sentence of Death: Lynching in the South* (Chapel Hill: University of North Carolina Press, 1997). Crystal Nicole Feimster, *Southern Horrors: Women and the Politics of Rape and*

Ralph Ellison called the white desire to rid the nation of its African-descended population "the fantasy of a blackless America."[7] This fantasy goes all the way back to the Founders. Thomas Jefferson first proposed the deportation of ex-slaves back to Africa in the late 18th century. In 1816, a group called the American Colonization Society put this vision into practice with financial support from federal appropriations. Black people, especially in the first generation after slavery, quietly turned repatriation to Africa to their own liberationist purposes. About 15,000 people left the U.S. for the west African country of Liberia, founded to receive them in 1847.[8]

After the Civil War, the "Jim Crow" laws that excluded Black citizens from the political sphere also involved corrupt law enforcement and expressed the psychological need to "purge" the United States of "blackness." The term

---

Lynching (Cambridge, Mass: Harvard University Press, 2009). James Goodman, *Stories of Scottsboro* (New York: Pantheon Books, 1994). Claude A. Clegg, *Troubled Ground: A Tale of Murder, Lynching, and Reckoning in the New South*, (Urbana: University of Illinois Press, 2010).

7 Ralph Ellison, "What America would be like without Blacks," in *Going to the Territory* (New York: Vintage International, 1986), 104.

8 Claude A. Clegg, *The Price of Liberty: African Americans and the Making of Liberia* (Chapel Hill: University of North Carolina Press, 2004); Marie Tyler-McGraw, *An African Republic: Black & White Virginians in the Making of Liberia*, (Chapel Hill: University of North Carolina Press, 2007).

"Redemption" was used by white supremacists to describe the removal of Black voters (and usually the Republican party as well) from the states of the former Confederacy after Reconstruction. The first generation after slavery worked hard to make good on their freedom, and a significant number of men were elected to public office as Republicans. "Redemption" is the white supremacists' word for pushing back on these gains. The word has religious overtones and evokes the idea of a rescue of the white population from "Negro domination" in politics. In the South, Redemption involved everything from election fraud to outright murder, culminating infamously in the military coup at Wilmington, North Carolina in 1898.[9] Of course, Oklahoma was not a state in the nineteenth century. As scholar Michell Wallace noted: Oklahoma whitened late.[10]

---

9 David S. Cecelski, Timothy B. Tyson, and John Hope Franklin, *Democracy Betrayed: The Wilmington Race Riot of 1898 and Its Legacy* (Chapel Hill: University of North Carolina Press, 1998); J. Morgan Kousser, *The Shaping of Southern Politics: Suffrage Restriction and the Establishment of the One-Party South, 1880-1910*, (New Haven: Yale University Press, 1974). Michael Perman, *The Road to Redemption: Southern Politics, 1869-1879* (Chapel Hill: University of North Carolina Press, 1984). Carole Emberton, *Beyond Redemption: Race, Violence, and the American South after the Civil War* (Chicago: The University of Chicago Press, 2013).

10 Michele Wallace, *Invisibility Blues: From Pop to Theory* (New York: Verso, 1990), 99. Wallace taught at the University of Oklahoma in the 1980s.

The poll tax, literacy test, grandfather clause, and "white primary" laws passed at the turn of the 20th century were states' retrospective legal bandages over the wounds of Reconstruction's violent undoing by "Redemption" in the 1880s and 1890s.[11] In the states of the former Confederacy, Jim Crow laws in politics created highly exclusionary one-party rule. These states radically shrank their electorates because poor whites, as well as Blacks, lost the vote due to the poll tax and literacy requirements. These states also tended to run weak, non-issue driven campaigns, and generally reduced the Republicans to a non-party. Between 1890 and the 1970s, the southern Democratic "party" was not really a mechanism for selecting candidates, identifying issues, and soliciting voters at all. As one political scientist put it recently, "The one-party South really had no political parties." Instead, the states of the former Confederacy after 1900 functioned as "subnational authoritarian enclaves" that kept the bulk of the population in line through violence, both real and threatened, and limited the power to rule to a small planter-industrial elite.[12]

---

[11] Michael Perman, *Struggle for Mastery: Disfranchisement in the South, 1888-1908* (Chapel Hill: University of North Carolina Press, 2001); C. Vann Woodward, *The Strange Career of Jim Crow*, (New York: Oxford University Press, 1955).

[12] Robert Mickey, *Paths out of Dixie: The Democratization of Authoritarian Enclaves in America's Deep South, 1944-1972* (Princeton, New Jersey: Princeton University Press, 2015), chapter 2.

But the border states like Tennessee and frontier states like Texas did not function like the deep South. In Texas, despite being a former Confederate State with a poll tax and white primary law, African Americans both voted and fought suffrage limitations all the way to the Supreme Court. The decision Smith v. Albright (1945) declaring the white primary law unconstitutional for the nation was brought against Texas by Black activists in the state and the NAACP. Like Oklahoma, Texas nestled its racist exclusion laws in the state constitution. Both states were vulnerable to federal court challenges because the U.S. Constitution guarantees each state a "Republican form of government." Between 1905 and 1945, Texas white county officials failed or only loosely enforced electoral restrictions and white candidates for office actively solicited the Black vote. White candidates or the parties paid the poll tax for Black voters, despite efforts to outlaw such behavior by the Texas legislature. With fourteen Black majority counties, a large Mexican American population, and significant German immigrant enclaves, the Republican party in Texas also hung on in key cities and counties. In this setting of competitive politics, Black voters remained vital as swing voters, if not on exactly their own terms.[13]

---

13 Darlene Clark Hine and Steven F. Lawson, *Black Victory: The Rise and Fall of the White Primary in Texas*, (Columbia: University of Missouri Press, 2003), chapter 2.

Similar conditions occurred in Oklahoma, a diverse, factionalized state with a very unstable two-party system. The first governor, Charles Haskell, sounded very much like a Democrat from the former Confederacy. At statehood in 1907, he declared that "Oklahoma will be a white man's state," and advocated Black exclusion from politics so that the population would "never bear the blight of negro domination."[14] Like other white demagogues in the Deep South, Haskell had a rather odd definition of the word "domination." They argued that Black swing votes somehow dictated election outcomes for the white majority, thereby "dominating" that population. What he meant was that Blacks held the potential "swing vote" in highly contested Oklahoma elections, such that their vote must be rigorously suppressed.

After Oklahoma statehood was approved by President Roosevelt in 1907, the first legislature engineered Black exclusion from the electorate with a grandfather clause. This clause stipulated that if one's grandfather had not voted before 1866, you could not vote in Oklahoma. Since enslaved people were not citizens and could not vote at that time, the clause effectively barred Black citizens from the ballot box. As in Texas, Black Oklahomans fought back. The case of Guinn v. Oklahoma was

---

14 "Roasts Negro Equality," *Guthrie Daily Ledger* (August 25, 1907), 2.

brought in 1911. The NAACP filed its first-ever amicus brief in support, and the case was eventually decided by the Supreme Court, which struck down the grandfather clause in 1915. [15]

Black voters in Jim Crow states had to make a choice. They could boycott elections and steer clear of registration and the polls and thereby protect their dignity and physical safety. Boycott could be a form of passive resistance. Or, they could attempt to register by paying the poll tax and passing the literacy test, even if their ballots were to be thrown out by law (as in Texas). This choice was more active resistance and it made registering into a political act. Black voters in Alabama, Virginia, Tennessee, and Texas took the active form of resistance to Jim Crow and participated in the political process through registration and, when possible, voting. They did so in Oklahoma as well.[16] Registering in Texas could at least protect one's ballot from being stolen by a white voter. Deep south states absorbed registration into the state apparatus, so citizens had to physically go to city hall to register, which

---

15 Anthony Hendricks, "Guinn v. U.S.: State's Rights and the 15th Amendment," *Oklahoma Bar Association* (blog), May 4, 2021, https://www.okbar.org/barjournal/may-2021/hendricks-2021/. (viewed 6-15-2023).

16 R. Darcy, "Did Oklahoma African Americans Vote Between 1910 and 1943?" *Chronicles of Oklahoma* 93, no. 1 (Spring 2015), 72-98.

could be very intimidating. But in other states, parties or candidates hired registrars to enroll voters out in the neighborhoods.[17]

Registrar was one of the few low-level patronage jobs that parties could distribute at campaign time to Black citizens, and this was the case in Oklahoma. The catch here was that Black neighborhoods were stigmatized by the "vice" establishments which were unfairly segregated into their environs, so registration activity was carried out in the shadow of law-breaking and corruption. By raising suspicions about the integrity of the registration process in the press, Democrats could suppress voter turnout, which tended to advantage their side. The *Tulsa Tribune* precisely tried these tactics during the primaries in the spring of 1920. "The democrats cannot find [registrars] with any greater degree of success than the republicans," noted one article, speculating that registrars drifted away from their posts in the neighborhoods out of boredom, preferring "to watch the streetcars breeze by" or out of a "hankering for near beer."[18]

One of the leading voices for Black political participation in Tulsa before the Massacre was that of An-

---

17 Volney Riser, *Defying Disfranchisement: Black Voting Rights Activism in the Jim Crow South, 1890-1908* (Baton Rouge: LSU Press, 2010).

18 "Voters have three more days for Registration," *Tulsa Tribune* (4 March 1920), 4.

drew J. Smitherman. Smitherman was born in 1885 in Childersburg, Alabama, Talladega County. His mother was a schoolteacher, and his father was an enterprising coal miner who ran a substantial charcoal manufacturing business. Smitherman was a small boy when the family moved to Indian Territory, where his father worked in Lehigh, a mining town 15 miles east of Atoka. His mother was determined that Andrew be educated, and he was sent to boarding school in Iowa. After graduation he moved to Muskogee, which in 1909 had a significant Black population. Smitherman offered his services to W. H. Twine, a family friend who was a lawyer and publisher of the Muskogee *Cimiter* newspaper.

In addition to transforming the *Cimiter* from a lackluster Republican sheet into a profitable newspaper, Smitherman became a great organizer of people and a tireless advocate for racial justice. He founded the Negro Guardianship League to correct the abuses of an Oklahoma law that permitted the appointment of guardians to minor children who had been allotted lands under the Dawes Act. Smitherman successfully redirected more than twenty guardianships back to their rightful owners and away from white crooks.[19] A vocal opponent of

---

19 "The Great Oil Boom," (10 September 1960), 5; "Thirteenth installment," (10 December 1960), 10. "The Great Steal" (12 November 1960), 5. "Rentie in the Clutches of the Law" (19 November 1960), 5. "Rentie Vindicated" (26 November 1960), 7, all in *Empire Star* [Buffalo, NY].

lynching, he put his own life in danger when he spoke out against racial violence in the press, confronted several mobs himself, and met with the governor of Oklahoma about the issue regardless of whether the victim was Black or white.[20]

In 1910, he married Olive Murphy, a farm girl from Arkansas who was skilled in the economics and practicalities of household management. The marriage was a devoted partnership and the two raised a large family, naming their first-born son Toussaint for Toussaint Louverture, hero of Black independence in Haiti. Smitherman's political coming of age involved a break with his employer and mentor in Muskogee. W.H. Twine was a dedicated Republican and, like his own father, was committed to the Party of Lincoln and the heritage of emancipation. But Smitherman believed that if Black voters stayed fixed in the Republican column, they would be "an open target in warfare between the two parties." Smitherman also witnessed Twine's friendships with Democrats from whom he "sought and obtained favors, big favors, many of them purely political." He could not understand why his mentor did not engage in "reciprocity" with his Democratic friends at election time. To meet these chang-

---

20 "Smitherman Writes Governor, Says Brother John was a Democrat," *Black Dispatch* [Oklahoma City] (23 March 1922), 1- 2.

ing conditions, Smitherman endorsed "diversifying" the Black vote, which placed Black voters as independent and forthright participants in democracy rather than as fixed partisans. "I still maintained that the logical thing for our group to do was to become diversified in politics," he argued, recommending that Black voters "join both parties and become a potent factor in elections by reason of our political diversification."[21] Twine worried that "old Satan" himself was behind this kind of thinking, but Smitherman was convinced that "our group had friends in both parties" so he joined the Democrats, moved to Tulsa, and in 1913 started his own newspaper *The Tulsa Star*.[22] From there, he worked to grow Black membership in the Democratic party.

After the Supreme Court overturned the grandfather clause in 1915, Black voting took on new life in Oklahoma. White leadership still tried to throw up roadblocks, but Smitherman moved forward with his vision of "independent" Black voting.[23] He did so out of racial pride. "No colored man whether democrat or republican can well afford to put the interest of any political party above that

---

21 "20th installment" *Empire Star* (28 January 1961),:10.

22 "Parting of the Ways," (25 February 1961): 10 and "The Grandfather clause" (1 October 1960), 5, both in *Empire Star*.

23 "Has no fear of negro vote," *Oklahoma City Times* (15 November 1915), 2.

3.1 Tulsa Star Masthead

of his race," he stated, adding that "We should remember we were Negroes before we were republicans or democrats."²⁴ By 1920, Democrats courted Black votes to beat Republicans at the local level in Tulsa. For example, the *Tulsa Tribune* reported on the nearly 200 participants at the "Negro Democratic State Convention" meeting at the Masonic Hall in the fall of 1920.²⁵ Then as now, the Republican party was the party of big business. Tulsa was dominated by oil magnates and industrialists who historically saw their interests in alignment with the Republicans.²⁶ For its part, the Republican commitment to

---

24 Editorial squib, *Tulsa Star* (30 September 1916), 4.

25 "Negro Democrats Plan Convention," *Tulsa Tribune* (30 September 1920), 4; "Negro Democrats Open State Meet," Tulsa Tribune (2 October 1920), 2; "Negro Democrats for Party Success," Tulsa Tribune (3 October 1920), 3. See also "Republicans Hold Convention Monday" and "Colored Democrats Meet Here" both in *Tulsa Star* (2 October 1920), 1.

26 James R. Scales, *Oklahoma Politics: A History* (Norman: University of Oklahoma Press, 1982), 97-117. Danney Goble, "Oklahoma Politics and the Sooner Electorate," in *Oklahoma Politics: New Views of the*

civil rights waned in the later 1910s, with no supportive planks in their platform and, by 1920, not even one Black delegate was seated at the Republican National Convention. Today, the party hosts the hard right, fascists, and outright racists.[27]

Smitherman was threading a needle since neither political party was a reliable ally of Black rights. He also had to know that in Texas and Tennessee, Black voters were inveigled into corrupt or compromising means to participate electorally. Robert Church, real estate magnate in Memphis, was a Black Republican leader who worked with the Democratic "machine" led by Edward Crump, shepherding Black votes on election day for money, federal appointments, and other favors.[28] The question for Smitherman then was how to get beyond "individual selfishness" in politics, to serve "the common good," and to generate electoral leverage for Black voters honestly

---

Forty-Sixth State, eds. Anne Hodes Morgan and H. Wayne Morgan (Norman: University of Oklahoma Press, 1982), 134-150.

27 Chris Danielson, ""Lily White and Hard Right": The Mississippi Republican Party and Black Voting, 1965-1980," *The Journal of Southern History* 75, no. 1 (2009), 83-118.

28 Republican stalwart Robert R. Church's long career in Memphis is well documented in Elizabeth Gritter, *River of Hope: Black Politics and the Memphis Freedom Movement, 1865-1954* (Lexington, Kentucky: University Press of Kentucky, 2014), chapters 2 and 3.

in Tulsa.[29]

In the lead up to the 1920 elections, Smitherman stressed two things. One was the proper registration of voters in the 23rd electoral ward, which encompassed Greenwood. Hand in glove with election integrity was the addition of women voters after the suffrage amendment passed 1919. For many years, suffragists argued that women could "clean up" politics and improve the tone of partisan elections mainly through their support of prohibition. Since drinking and saloon life was part of male-dominated party politics, moving registration stations out of saloons and into "dry" spaces was seen as a hedge against corruption at the ballot box and a way to make politics more welcoming for women citizens and, overall, fairer for everyone.

Smitherman's *Tulsa Star* beat the drum of honest registration in Greenwood. His wife was noted to be the chair of the entertainment committee for the Negro Democratic Club; her presence and that of other ladies at meetings evoked sobriety and respectability. Smitherman took pains to describe how voters registered in Greenwood. At the Red Wing Cafe, proprietor Julius.T. Pressly also worked as a registrar. A young lady "suffrag-

---

29 "The Parting of the Ways," *Empire Star* [Buffalo, NY] (25 February 1961), 10

ette" sitting at an "immaculate white table" was properly registered by him, including "record[ing] the color of the skin."³⁰ Women were described as model citizens. On election day, a beloved community member named Mrs. Marshall was carried in a chair from her sick bed to the polls, such was her devotion to exercising her new right to vote.³¹ In the general election in the fall, an article under a banner headline "Women to Rebuke Republicans" in the *Star* explained that Black women voters should punish the city administration for the wrongful arrest and maltreatment of another community member named Mrs. Parker, who was detained overnight in jail. Smitherman commended the women who refused to be "the tools of the G.O.P."³²

The *Star* also highlighted "independent" rather than strictly partisan voting by Black citizens. Smitherman boasted that in Tulsa, "probably the colored people in no other city in the country are so happily diversified in politics" between the two parties.³³ Smitherman and his good friend J.B. Stradford, a very wealthy hotelier, modeled a

---

30 "Just a Straight Democrat, Please" *Tulsa Star* (27 March 1920), 1.

31 "Woman leaves bed to vote for Hubbard," *Tulsa Star* (10 April 1920), 11.

32 "Women to Rebuke Republicans," *Tulsa Star* (30 October 1920), 1.

33 "Colored Women as Democrats," *Tulsa Star* (6 March 1920,: 8.

bipartisan electoral strategy. Stradford was a Republican and ran for city commissioner on the Republican ticket in the 1920 spring primary. Stradford and Smitherman modeled ticket-splitting, as both endorsed the incumbent Mayor Charles Hubbard (a Democrat) for mayor of Tulsa that year.[34]

According to the white press, Hubbard was defeated mostly by defections of lily white Democrats to the Republican column for mayor in the general election.[35] Smitherman's *Tulsa Star* headline pointed out proudly that Hubbard only lost by 206 votes, which perfectly made his point about the decisive difference a well-organized swing group of voters could make in the highly competitive Tulsa political scene.[36] The importance of swing voters was never more evident than in the 1920 city election. By a razor margin, the incumbent mayor who had campaigned in Greenwood and who was a supporter of A. J. Smitherman was removed from office. His place was taken by a Republican mayor who oversaw the Tulsa Race Massacre.

---

34 "Popular Colored Republican Candidate Praises City Democratic Administration," *Tulsa Star* (13 March 1920), 1.

35 "Evans and Bigger Tulsa Ticket Win," *Tulsa Daily World* (7 April 1920), 1.

36 "Republicans Win by 206 Votes!" *Tulsa Star* (10 April 1920), 1.

Smitherman continued to promote his theme of independent voting in the run up to the general and presidential elections in the fall of 1920. Though the Republicans swept the national elections, the *Tulsa Star* editor was "ecstatic over the triumph of the policies it has so faithfully and earnestly advocated...that the votes of the Race should be divided between the two great parties" and that "colored candidates" should be represented on both tickets.[37]

Smitherman and Stradford were far from alone in their approach to independent voting. Attorney B. C. Franklin was a proud "Negro Democrat" in Oklahoma in the 1910s. This affiliation made him very unpopular with his neighbors in all-Black Rentiesville, but later they hailed him as a "prophet."[38] Since the late nineteenth century, Black leadership had advocated tactical partisanship, policy-driven voting behaviors, and even a "Negro Party" to protect Black voters from overdependence on the Republican party which too often betrayed them.[39] The

---

37 "Wherein the Tulsa Star Scratches Its Own Back," *Tulsa Star* (30 October 1920), 1.

38 Buck Colbert Franklin, *My Life and an Era: The Autobiography of Buck Colbert Franklin* (Baton Rouge: Louisiana State University Press, 1997), 190-191.

39 Stephen Robinson, "'To Think, Act, Vote, and Speak for Ourselves': Black Democrats and Black 'Agency' in the American South after Reconstruction," *Journal of Social History* 48, no. 2 (2014), 363-82.

3.2 *The Tulsa Star* (Tulsa, Okla.)
Vol. 9, No. 12, Ed. 1, Saturday, April 10, 1920

strongest voices for political independence for Black voters came, perhaps not surprisingly, from New York City. Activist editor T. Thomas Fortune argued that "colored Americans should be independent voters, independent citizens, independent men."[40] In the years around World War I, W.E.B. Du Bois despaired that Black voters felt "politically helpless" and were given "no choice" between the parties at election time.[41] Citing Smitherman, political scientists now identify 1916 as an early turning point in the disaffection of Black voters from the Republican party to the Democrats.[42]

Nonetheless, A.J. Smitherman walked a tightrope. White supremacists in Tulsa propagandized the notion that Black voters were either blindly loyal to the Republican party, were "herded" to the ballot box by political handlers, or were easily purchased by the Democrats, whom

---

Bruce L. Mouser, *For Labor, Race, and Liberty George Edwin Taylor, His Historic Run for the White House, and the Making of Independent Black Politics* (Madison, Wis: University of Wisconsin Press, 2011).

40 T. Thomas Fortune, *Black and White: Labor and Politics in the South* (1884; reprint New York 1968), chapter 6.

41 W. E. B. Du Bois, *Dusk of Dawn: An Essay toward an Autobiography of a Race Concept*, (New York: Harcourt, Brace and Co., 1940), 241.

42 David Oks, "The Election of 1916, 'Negrowumpism,' and the Black Defection from the Republican Party," *The Journal of the Gilded Age and Progressive Era* 20, no. 4 (2021), 523–47.

they would (supposedly) backstab on election day.⁴³ The other important racist reflex among whites in Oklahoma was the association of the African American community with vice, especially liquor consumption. This association was also supremely self-serving since as a "dry" state, no one was supposed to buy or sell liquor on the open market in Oklahoma (though it was available medicinally). Alcohol and commercial vice were significantly segregated into Greenwood. The few appointive offices available to Black men were as lower-level law enforcement agents, like deputy sheriff or justice of the peace.⁴⁴ Since Blacks rarely, if ever policed white neighborhoods, the association with corruption, the vice economy, and Greenwood was reinforced many times over. It bears mentioning that of the many and persistent violations Oklahomans made of their own prohibition laws in these years, the city of Tulsa was the worst offender of all.⁴⁵

Thus, when white Tulsa electoral candidates cam-

---

43 "Tossing the Bait to African Voters," *Tulsa Daily World* (12 September 1915), 5. "Has no fear of negro vote," *Oklahoma City Times* (1 November 1915), 2.

44 "Race Man Appointed Justice of the Peace," *Tulsa Star* (10 April 1920), 11.

45 James Edward Klein, "A Social History of Prohibition in Oklahoma, 1900-1920," (MA, University of Iowa, 2003), 137-165. Jimmie Lewis Franklin, *Born Sober: Prohibition in Oklahoma, 1907-1959* (Norman: University of Oklahoma Press, 1971).

paigned on "good government" and "clean elections," their words could always be read as code for regulating and punishing the Black community. To push back, Smitherman worked hard to unpack the association of vice, political corruption, and the Black vote in Greenwood. Through the *Tulsa Star*, he created a public counter narrative about cleaning up vice dens and prostitution (the latter involving white women, he pointed out), as well as "blind pigs" (illegal establishments that sold alcohol). He managed to have the public library branch sited in the *Tulsa Star* office, thus reinforcing the idea of a civic-minded Greenwood.[46] The white supremacist opposition took a predictable stance. After abetting the Massacre that killed hundreds of people and leveled the churches, homes, and businesses in Greenwood, the *Tulsa Tribune* editorialized that "N----rtown must never be allowed in Tulsa again" since it was full of "booze, dope, bad n---s, and guns."[47] This racist sentiment echoed in national contexts as well. After slandering the Greenwood Black community as nothing but a "N---rtown," an influential

---

46 Barbara A. Seals Nevergold, "A. J. Smitherman: Pen Warrior," *Chronicles of Oklahoma* 89, no. 3 (2011), 288-311. Myrna Magliulo, "Andrew J. Smitherman: A Pioneer of the African American Press, 1909-1961," *Afro-Americans in New York Life and History* 34, no. 2 (2010), 119-53.

47 "It Must Not Be Again," *Tulsa Tribune* (4 June 1921), 8.

writer from Philadelphia also called out the city of Tulsa as a "crook's paradise," that was "more indifferent to law enforcement than other cities" in the United States.[48]

Smitherman and independent Black voting in Tulsa may not have had power "over" the white community *per se*, but the 1920 elections signaled that neither could Black citizens in Greenwood be controlled. The vote of an 'uncontrolled" Black voter took on added significance when conservative white voters shifted toward the Republican Party, thus offsetting the Democrats' large lead in registered voters. In May 1920, Police Commissioner J.M. Adkinson sought to filter out any political conflicts of interest. The department created a merit application blank where the applicant had to truthfully and honestly state whether or not they were republican, democrat, or socialist. Self-determination was a beacon that could no longer be disregarded.[49] The political flame would become even brighter leading up to the 1920 Presidential election.

The Greenwood community further declared its independence when men showed up at the jail after Dick Rowland was arrested on an assault charge on May 31,

---

[48] Amy Comstock, " 'Over Time': Another view of the Tulsa Riots," *Survey* 46 (2 July 1921), 460.

[49] "City Police Take Oath Under Evans," *Tulsa Tribune*, May 5, 1920, 1.

1921. Their purpose was to protect his safety while in custody, given that lynching rumors were already rife. In contrast to the prevailing narrative that Dick Rowland was barricaded within the courthouse premises, shielded by six deputies, Sheriff's Deputy Barney Cleaver, in an interview with *The Black Dispatch* newspaper, later stated: "he (Rowland) was not in the jail when the mob appeared there." There is a general consensus that the occurrence of violence that began on May 31st was inevitable. Nevertheless, concealing the fact that Dick Rowland was absent from the courthouse "before the mob appeared there" once again demonstrates the culpability of law enforcement.

One could contend that withholding this information violated their oath to support, obey, and defend the U. S. and State Constitutions, as well as Tulsa's ordinances and charter. The residents of America's Black Wall Street would not have their constitutional rights protected. The Fourteenth Amendment's Section 1 definition of equal protection under the law is unambiguous.

All persons born or naturalized in the United States, and subject to the jurisdiction thereof, are citizens of the United States and of the state wherein they reside. No state shall make or enforce any law which shall abridge the privileges or immunities of citizens of the United States; nor shall any state deprive any person of life, liberty, or property, without due process of law; nor deny to any person within its jurisdiction the equal protection of the laws.

In the interview with *The Black Dispatch*, Cleaver further states "They could not afford to tell where he (Rowland) was," On two separate occasions, African American Patriots were willing to put their lives on the line to offer Sheriff Willard McCullough their assistance in protecting the courthouse. A good many of them were veterans of World War I who had also taken an oath to defend the Constitution of the United States of America against tyranny both at home and abroad. They should have been exempt from the conspiracy of silence that had kept them ignorant of the fact that they were defending an illusion. From the perspective of those who survived the Massacre, the cost of this silence was the utter annihilation of America's Black Wall Street. It is necessary to ask critical questions. Was it a conscious decision to forego an opportunity for de-escalation, or was it an opportunity to launch a more calculated and diabolical clash of the races?

3.3 "A Descriptive Poem of the Tulsa Riot and Massacre," 1921. A.J. Smitherman (seated) with his wife Olive Murphy Smitherman and their five children (Beinecke Rare Book and Manuscript Library, Yale University)

Among the cruelest ironies of the Tulsa Race Massacre is the indictment of at least 56 Black men, including Smitherman and Stradford, for rioting and the unlawful use of firearms. In the immediate aftermath of the Massacre, Smitherman and his family found temporary refuge in Minneapolis and Boston. There, the Black community and NAACP activists provided shelter and advocacy. NAACP lawyers successfully engaged with the Minnesota Attorney General to convince the governor of Minnesota not to sign extradition papers.[50] Tulsa never came after him. Similarly, Dick Rowland's grand jury indictment for attempted rape and assault was dismissed after the supposed victim, a white woman named Sarah Page, refused to press charges. On September 28, 1921, Page failed to appear for a court docket call, and the case was dismissed. In the

> Dick Rowland, according to Barney Cleaver, who was in Oklahoma City Sunday, on his way to Granite with prisoners, IS IN SOUTH OMAHA. He was released by the Tulsa authorities no charges ever being placed against him. This bears out the statement of the Black Dispatch that the mob of white hoodlums at the jail were attempting to murder an innocent man. "HE WAS NOT IN THE JAIL WHEN THE MOB APPEARED THERE," said Cleaver, "but we could not afford to tell where he was. Sarah Page has vanished as completely as a mirage on a desert. The story still stands that all that Dick Rowland was guilty of was stumbling and stepping on the foot of Sarah Page. She struck him with her hand bag, he grabbed her hand as he stepped out of the elevator.

3.4 *The Black Dispatch*
Vol. 6, No. 28, Ed. 1
Friday, June 17, 192

50 Assistant Secretary to Gov. J.A.O. Preus, 20 October 1921 and James Markham to Hon. S.P. Freeling 31 October 1921, Extradition of Chas. T. Smitherman, 1922 file in Group I, series D, legal files (Extraditions, 1920-1935), viewed online through History Vault: NAACP (6-24-2013).

same month, Page married Fred E. Voorhies, who, ironically, was a co-witness in the grand jury investigation that led to Rowland's indictment.[51]

White Tulsa had no actual "case" against the Black community in Greenwood, but neither could they control them politically.[52] This lack of control manifested itself as lethal white rage. A final example makes the point.

The Massacre had driven A. J. Smitherman out of Oklahoma, but his younger brother John or J. H., remained in Tulsa. J. H. Smitherman was in law enforcement, including serving as a Tulsa County deputy Sheriff during the Massacre. He had also been indicted for inciting "the riot" by the all-white grand jury, charges which were later dropped.

On March 9, 1922, a front page article in the *Tulsa Tribune* once again preceded atrocity. Tulsa's biannual municipal elections were a month away and a sudden panic had ensued in the political classes regarding Black voter registration. The Republicans who ran the City during

---

51 Randy Hopkins, "The Notorious Sarah Page," https://www.centerforpublicsecrets.org/post/the-notorious-sarah-page

52 Randy Hopkins, "The Plot to Kill 'Diamond Dick' Rowland and the Tulsa Race Massacre," *The Chronicles of Oklahoma* vol. 99, 1 (Spring 2021), 4-49; Alfred L. Brophy, *Reconstructing Dreamland: The Tulsa Riot of 1921: Race, Reparations, and Reconciliation* (New York: Oxford University Press, 2002), 179.

the Massacre were worried about a rising wave of Black voters no longer in thrall to the GOP. White Democrats had mixed feelings as well. The *Tribune* pinned a bulls-eye on John Smitherman by reporting that he had "admitted that he had urged the negro electors to register as Democrats" and that he registered "bootleggers, dope heads and prostitutes."[53]

The next day, Smitherman was awakened in the middle of the night by pounding on his door. He was confronted by armed, masked men who claimed to be policemen and who wore police badges. Sticking pistols in his ribs, they demanded that he accompany them to the police station. Smitherman demanded to see a warrant, but none was produced.

Instead, Smitherman was forced into a car at gunpoint, blindfolded, and driven out of town in a caravan carrying twelve white men, most of whom were masked. He was stripped, chained to a tree, beaten, spat upon and beaten some more. The attackers accused him of "registering them damn negroes as Democrats and telling them to vote against this present city administration, which is for good government." In his testimony during a Klan inves-

---

53 "Registration in some precincts held illegal," *Tulsa Tribune* (10 March 1922), 1-2. "Unmasked band abducts negro and white man," *Tulsa Tribune* (11 March 1922), 1.

tigation carried out by Governor Walton in 1923, Smitherman explained that a well-dressed white man — "this little fellow" — pulled a gun, stuck it to Smitherman's head and screamed, "I am going to kill you." Dissuaded from taking this final step, the diminutive madman pulled a knife, caught hold of Smitherman's left ear, and sliced, boasting as he did that he would make Smitherman, "a marked mother sucker the balance of [his] life." Not bothering to wear a mask, the pin-stripped sadist tried to make Smitherman eat his own ear, pistol-whipping him when he refused. Smitherman was finally cut loose from his bonds, ordered to leave Oklahoma never to return, and then abandoned in the dark woods. Smitherman's description of his primary torturer was said to minutely fit one "Shorty" Mondier, a security guard at the Mid-Continent Building and a plainclothes detective for the Tulsa Police Department.[54]

This hideous account is rife with white supremacist behaviors and rituals. The idea that any group of white men could police and punish a Black man comes directly out of slavery, when slaves had no protection

---

54 "J.H. Smitherman Case," John C. Walton Collection, The Western History Collections, University of Oklahoma, box 14, folder 21. "Negro Whipped, one ear cut off by masked band," *Tulsa Daily World* (12 March 1922), 1. "White Band Whips Negro, cuts off ear," *Tulsa Tribune* (12 March 1922), 1.

3.6 *The Morning Tulsa Daily World (Tulsa, Oklahoma) · Sun, Mar 12, 1922 · Page 1*

as citizens who were innocent until proven guilty. The Tulsa attackers added "ungentlemanly conduct towards a white woman" to the list of alleged transgressions by Smitherman, the old lie that led to lynchings. The Walton investigation revealed that the charge regarding the white woman was baseless. She herself confirmed it.[55]

Lynching victims were often castrated or maimed. Severed body parts were then either stuffed into the victim's mouth or placed on display after death (or both). In this case, the mob took an ear. Notching an ear is practiced in animal husbandry and used on pigs and cows. The ear of the bull is awarded as a prize to a matador after a bullfight. Rebellious slaves had their ears "bored" or notched to mark them as troublemakers. Rooted in the dehumanizing practices of slavery, the maiming of John Smitherman represents the brute impulse of a white man to "mark" a Black man as a subordinate for the rest of his life. And yet the political charges stand out in this grisly

---

55 "J.H. Smitherman Case," John C. Walton Collection, Western History Collections.

narrative: registering and party affiliation were Smitherman's primary "crimes."

This white mob had to reach back to slavery's protocols to try and defeat the Smithermans of Tulsa. The Smithermans represented the Black voice and the Black vote. The historic violent response to black political enfranchisement reveals that the Black vote has always been one of the greatest threats to the idea of white supremacy and social control. No one should wonder why voter suppression and other unethical forms of voter intimidation still exist today. The legacy of Jim Crow still holds hostage those who wish to maintain a system that is eating away the very soul of America.

CHAPTER FOUR

Testifying to Atrocity

> *"It is incredible that this must be said, but the obvious seems to escape politicized academics, so we must state the obvious: Genocide is deliberate; it is premeditated."* There is no genocide without premeditation. The murders are not unfortunate coincidences. This is why it is called "mass MURDER" and not "mass MANSLAUGHTER."
>
> —A.E. Samaan

The white authorities of the time acknowledged the obvious central responsibility for the Tulsa Race Massacre from the beginning. On June 1, 1921, after most of the damage had been done, Oklahoma National Guard Adjutant General Charles F. Barrett declared martial law and took control of the City. The day after Greenwood's incineration, Barrett addressed a meeting of top drawer Tulsa businessmen of the Tulsa Chamber of Commerce at city hall. He lambasted Tulsa city and county officials who had "simply laid down." He would later write that the Tulsa police department's hundreds of special deputies formed "the most dangerous part of the mob."[1] At Barrett's urging, the Chamber created a committee to take control of the City from elected officials and help clean up the mess. A former Tulsa mayor, Loyal J. Martin, declared, "the city and county is (sic) legally liable for every dollar of the damage which has been done." "Smashing applause" greeted Martin's speech and he was unanimously elected head of a committee called the Bureau of Public Welfare to oversee control of the thousands of Greenwood citizens who remained in concentration camps and to rebuild the ruins. Six bankers and oilmen made up the rest of the Bureau. One member, H. L. Standeven, President of the Exchange National Bank's trust company, said that all of Tulsa should bear the burden of reconstruction.[2]

Also on June 2, 1921, Major Alva Niles, President of the Tulsa Chamber of Commerce, issued a letter to the newspapers of the U. S. announcing a plan of "reparations in order that (Greenwood) homes may be rebuilt and families as nearly as possible rehabilitated." It was the

---

[1] "Tulsa Race Riot: A Report by the Oklahoma Commission to Study the Tulsa Race Riot of 1921, 159.

[2] "Tulsa Officials "Simply Laid Down,"" *Sapulpa (OK) Herald*, June 2, 1921, 1.

4.1 Courtesy of The Daily Oklahoman

first use of the word "reparations" in connection with the Tulsa Race Massacre and it came from the chief of white Tulsa's business establishment.³ News of the reparations plan dominated newspaper headlines from coast to coast and shoved news of the catastrophe itself down into the small print. Those national headlines made white Tulsa businessmen look heroic.

These same men escalated this vision of white heroism with a June 4, 1921 national pronouncement that all outside contributions to the rebuilding effort would be rejected. Sufficient funds, they boasted, could be obtained locally and that "Tulsa feels equal to the task of its own restitution."⁴

---

3 "Niles Blames Lawlessness For Race War," *Tulsa Tribune*, June 2, 1921, 4.

4 "Committee Can Raise Relief," *Post-Dispatch*, June 3, 1921, 1.

As soon as the favorable newspaper headlines were published, the "reparations" plan was dropped like a rock. There was no serious effort to collect rebuilding funds. The very word "reparations" vanished from the Tulsa lexicon for decades. It had all been a public relations operation executed by the Tulsa Chamber of Commerce.⁵ Instead, a vigorous campaign to deny and deflect responsibility was waged in the media. The facts themselves were spun to make white Tulsa appear justified in their behavior — it was all the fault of the "bad negroes." Even the insurance companies knew where to look for responsibility. While quick to deny their own liability for property and life insurance policies because of a "riot" exclusion, they directed frustrated policyholders to sue the city and county for "negligence" in the protection of property. Negligence on the part of city and county officials was obvious from the outset, but history shows that the Oklahoma legal system was incapable of delivering even a modicum of

4.1 The Morning Tulsa Daily World Thu, Jun 2, 1921 · Page 7

---

5 Randy Hopkins, "Mask of Atonement: Mark of the Hun" (2021). *The Tulsa Race Massacre: Teaching and Learning Resources* https://archives.pdx.edu/ds/psu/36427 (viewed 6-25-2023).

justice. The original suits were dismissed or failed.

The charges against the white perpetrators came to virtually nothing, as did the charges against falsely accused Black "rioters." They were all swept away in an effort to make everyone forget what had happened. After 1921, J. B. Stradford lived in exile until his death and eventually had his name cleared in 1996, thanks to advocacy by his family members.[6]

While the central responsibility for the Tulsa Race Massacre has been and remains beyond question, justice continues to elude Black Tulsans. This blockage is the result of 100 years of stubborn, cold-hearted, intergenerational refusal on the part of white Tulsans to take full responsibility for the crimes committed. While "facts" and "responsibility" may appear to be indistinguishable, this reality has been an obstacle for Black victims. In 2018, however, a fresh hope appeared out of nowhere. In response to a news story about Oaklawn Cemetery that Vanessa Hall Harper, Tulsa's sole African-American city councilor, had triggered, the City of Tulsa opened an official investigation into the mass graves long associated with the Massacre.

---

6 "Oklahoma clears Black in Deadly 1921 Race Riot," *New York Times* (26 October 1996), 8.

In announcing the Investigation, Tulsa's mayor G. T. Bynum used robust language. He promised that it would be conducted like a "homicide investigation." He declared a "compact" with the Massacre's murdered victims to get to the truth.[7]

At the urging of Hall-Harper, Bynum established a Public Oversight Committee consisting of descendants of Race Massacre victims and other influential members of Tulsa's African-American community. I was among those selected to serve. According to Bynum's words at the time, the Committee was to "oversee the project," to provide transparency, and to hold the City "accountable" for doing things "the right way." The Mayor promised that the Committee's role was to "point out (where) it isn't being done in the right way and where we need to be right."

Thereafter, technical experts were hired, and a series of tests were conducted in the City-owned Oaklawn Cemetery, one of the suspected locations of Massacre victims. In the late fall of 2020, a test excavation in Oaklawn's so-called Colored Potter's Field yielded the discovery of a mass grave, as the City's experts from the University of

---

7 Bynum quotation regarding "compact" from *Oaklawn* (documentary film) 2022. Randy Hopkins, "Echo of History: The City of Tulsa's Mass Graves Debacle," note 15 (viewed 6-24-2023) https://www.centerforpublicsecrets.org/post/echo-of-history-the-city-of-tulsa-s-mass-graves-debacle.

Oklahoma and The University of Florida proclaimed it. In early 2021, the Public Oversight Committee was called upon by Bynum to vote to approve a full excavation of the Oaklawn mass grave site. The Committee's unanimous approval was given in March 2021.

The City began excavations on June 1, 2021, the exact Centennial of the Massacre. Just as national attention was again focused on Tulsa, the turning of the ground in the City-owned cemetery was timed for maximum public impact. Once again, the City authorities were making themselves look good.

Over the course of three weeks, the excavations unearthed at least 35 sets of human remains, 19 of which were carefully exhumed. The Oversight Committee members solemnly transported to an on-site forensic laboratory for further study. This Oaklawn "dig" reached its zenith on June 23 with the discovery of human remains bearing evidence of gunshot trauma. Gunshot wounds were the gold standard for what the searchers were pursuing in terms of Massacre victims. Finally, after the long, tortuous, and traumatizing efforts, hope for at least some elemental justice — the finding of Massacre victims — flared brighter than ever. Little did we know that even that glimmer of hope was about to be smothered.

Quick rewind. The first round of Black defense after the Massacre in 1921 involved insurance claims and a legal fight against the city. Whites tried to prevent Blacks from rebuilding the burned out district through restrictive building codes and other policies designed to enable a land grab for developers. The idea from the City's perspective was to move the Black community further north and east of downtown. However, lawyer B.C. Franklin fought this maneuver and defeated some of this early attempt at "urban renewal" (the latter is sometimes referred to by Civil Rights activists as "Negro Removal"). Franklin's victory resulted in the establishment of a notable, albeit limited, foothold for the people who survived. An estimated 40% of Black Greenwood's original residents returned to rebuild.

In 1945, my grandfather, Raymond Beard returned to Tulsa after World War II and married Earna May Everidge. During the post-war period, the community did its best to oppose urban renewal initiatives that were similarly intended to benefit white economic development at the expense of the Black community's economic foothold. These conflicts were a mixed bag and led to the construction of a highway directly over the location of the Dreamland Theatre, which was owned by Loula and John Williams.[8] The highway still cuts like a knife right

---

8 Luckerson, *Built from Fire*, chapter 8. Greta K. Smith, " 'The Battling Ground:' Memory, Violence and Resistance in Greenwood, North Tulsa, Oklahoma, 1907-1980," (MA Thesis, Portland State University 2021).

4.2 May 4, 1967, Tulsa Tribune construction of the Crosstown Expressway and Interstate 244 in the Greenwood District. Courtesy of Tulsa Tribune and Tulsa City County Library

through the heart of Greenwood.

In 1982, Black Tulsans elected their own Representative to the Oklahoma state legislature, fueled by civil rights action in the 1960s. Don Ross was born in 1941 and, like me, attended Booker T. Washington High School before attending Central State University. He had been active in the Congress of Racial Equality during the 1960s, advocating for justice in housing, public accommodations, and employment. He also studied law and journalism and managed the *Oklahoma Eagle* newspaper in Tulsa for many years. As a legislator, he got the Confederate Flag removed from the state Capital's ground and made sure that Oklahoma proclaimed Martin Luther King Jr., Day as a national holiday (Reagan signed the bill in 1983). Ross also brought much needed attention to the Massacre and its buried history in the state. He developed legislation and secured funding for a new Greenwood Cultural Center, which opened in 1995.[9]

Don Ross helped bring the facts of the Massacre back into public view and public discussion. He was a role model at the time for other states seeking truth and reconciliation for racial injustices.[10] In 1999, he created legislation for a Commission charged with investigating the event and making recommendations to the Oklahoma legislature. The work of the 1921 Race Riot Commission was a chance for a new generation of Oklahomans to confront the facts and details of the atrocity, which were published in a 2001 report. Some of the Report's recom-

---

9 "Don Ross" in Uncrowned Community Builders Biographical Dictionary https://www.uncrownedcommunitybuilders.com/person/don-ross (viewed 6-21-2023).

10 See folders 3 and 10, Box 12, 1898 Foundation Papers, Center for Southeast North Carolina Archives & History, University of North Carolina, Wilmington.

mendations included direct payment of reparations to survivors of the Tulsa Race Riot, direct payment of reparations to descendants of the survivors of the Tulsa Race Riot, a scholarship fund available to students affected by the Tulsa Race Riot, the establishment of an economic development enterprise zone in the historic area of the Greenwood District, and a memorial for the reburial of any human remains found in the search for unmarked graves of riot victims. None of the recommendations have been resolved.

There now stands a "Black Wall Street Memorial" in Greenwood, a ten-foot granite monument that lists the names of the known businesses that existed in Greenwood before the Massacre. The names of some victims are engraved there, like those of Dr. A.C. Jackson. A college scholarship was established for descendants. Ross also spearheaded the 75th anniversary commemoration of the Massacre, which was then called a "race riot." Reparations were called for by the report, but scuttled by the Governor.[11] This is where the divide between facts and responsibility becomes painfully, unavoidably evident.

The findings in the Report and the fact that Massacre survivors were starting to age generated momentum

---

11 Ross E. Milloy, "Panel Calls for Reparations in Tulsa Race Riots," *New York Times* (1 March 2001), A12.

for another legal challenge. In 2002, the distinguished civil rights attorney, Charles R. Ogletree, Jr., best known for representing another famous Oklahoman, Anita Hill, came to University of Tulsa to give the Buck Colbert Franklin Memorial Lecture at the University of Tulsa School of Law. Ogletree was invited to the Greenwood Cultural Center during this visit and met with a group of community members for several hours. "The youngest person there was in his late 80s," he recalled. "The oldest was 105 years old." [12]

Olgetree understood that the "Tulsa victims never had a day in court to present their claims." He committed himself to righting this wrong. He assembled a team and, based on the Commission Report, argued that the statute of limitations defense, which was thought to block the bringing of civil charges, could be avoided. My grandfather was among the 150 plaintiffs named in this lawsuit, though he passed away before the case was decided in 2004. Ogletrees's team of litigators sought to "toll" the statute of limitations by activating the statutory provisions for doing so. Essentially, he argued that limitations could be tolled and a case brought forward in

---

12 Charles J. Ogletree, "History, Genius, and Unhealed Wounds After Tulsa's Race Riot," in *When Law Fails: Making Sense of Miscarriages of Justice* (New York: New York University Press, 2020), 57.

the presence of important new evidence. Federal Judge James Ellison of the Western District of Oklahoma gave a "stunningly sympathetic and technically narrow ruling," disagreeing that the 2001 Race Riot Commission Report met the legal threshold. A request for a rehearing in Oklahoma was denied. The petition to appear before the U.S. Supreme Court was refused "without a word or a hearing," noted Ogletree.[13]

A few years later, another wave of optimism surrounded the efforts of Congressman John Conyers of Michigan, the first African-American chair of the House Judiciary Committee. In 2007, Conyers convened hearings on the Tulsa riot, during which several Tulsans, including survivors, made the trek to Washington, D.C. Conyers also shepherded legislation, H.R. 1995, to extend the statute of limitations for five years to allow the Tulsa victims to mount a legal case. The bill was never passed.

Finally, on September 1, 2020, a lawsuit was brought on behalf of the remaining surviving Massacre victims, and others by Damario Solomon-Simmons, The case sought to avoid the limitation issue on the ground of a 'public nuisance' theory, one that had been used to avoid limitations in another case. The suit was filed in Oklahoma district court in Tulsa and made its way, very slowly,

---

13 Ibid., 58- 60.

through the Oklahoma state court system. Initially, state judge Caroline Wall ruled positively, but narrowly on the case. Most of the plaintiffs were dismissed, but the surviving victims of the massacre, Mother Viola Fletcher, Mother Lessie Benningfield Randle, and Hughes Van Ellis, Sr., were temporarily empowered to "proceed to discovery" and bring claims that the Massacre constitutes a "public nuisance" that continues to produce harm today.[14]

I hope you are asking: *"Nuisance?* Why not murder charges?" There is no statute of limitations on murder. Here is where some of the ugliest parts of white denial in the Massacre show up. The inability to bring murder charges was the direct result of malfeasance by officials in 1921. The links between the names of those who pulled the triggers and threw the torches and the bodies of the victims have been disrupted. Those are the basic building blocks of a criminal prosecution. The Tulsa Police failed to account for the names of the four hundred or so white "deputies" who were empowered to attack Greenwood on the morning of June 1, 1921.[15] At least 250 of those dep-

---

14 Justice for Greenwood press release, 4 August 1922. https://www.justiceforgreenwood.org/press-release-historic-court-ruling-last-living-survivors-of-1921-tulsa-race-massacre-entitled-to-prove-the-massacre-was-a-public-nuisance/. Viewed on 6-21-2023. On Friday, July 7th, 2023 the judge reversed herself and dismissed the case "with prejudiced. "

15 "Inefficiency of Police Is Denied, *Tulsa World*, July 19, 1921, 1,7.

uties had been armed by the police from weapons taken from downtown hardware stores, but we do not have their names, much less identifiers like the serial numbers of the guns so distributed.[16] Even more heinous was the destruction of other evidence, namely the bodies of the victims themselves. As already noted, most bodies were prepared and buried without death certificates. Delays and other irregularities surround the disposition of the dead.[17] The final report of the Red Cross, which took primary responsibility for relief and aid to Black victims for a full six months after the Massacre, omitted figures on the number of deaths, "for the reason that NO ONE KNOWS."[18]

16 For arming at least 250 men, deposition of J. A. Gustafson in *Stradford v. American Central Ins. Co.*, Superior Court of Cook County, no. 370, 274 (1922), 3-4 ("We armed during the night probably two hundred fifty citizens who assisted the Police Department in trying to quell the mob" and "I think we armed about two hundred fifty.").

17 Eddie Faye Gates, *Riot on Greenwood: The Total Destruction of Black Wall Street*, Illustrated edition (Austin, Tex: Eakin Press, 2003), 167. Clyde Collins Snow, "Confirmed Deaths: A Preliminary Report," *Tulsa Race Riot: A Report by the Oklahoma Commission to Study the Tulsa Race Riot of 1921* (28 February 2001), 109-122. It should be noted that the death of the perpetrators has forced any legal action around accountability to move through the civil side of the courts.

18 Red Cross Report, December 1921, Tulsa Historical Society https://www.tulsahistory.org/wp-content/uploads/2018/11/1921-Red-Cross-Report-December-30th.pdf viewed on 6-24-2023. Quotation from Maurice Willows to Mr. A.L. Farmer, 31 December 1921, 4 (viewed 6-24-2023), emphasis in original.

Fast forward. At 3:41 p.m. on May 18th, 2021, I received an urgent email requesting my testimony at a hearing in Washington, D.C., before the United States House Committee on the Judiciary Subcommittee on the Constitution, Civil Rights, and Civil Liberties. The email was from Driesen Heath, a highly sought-after researcher and advocate for the global justice organization Human Rights Watch. My heart began to race as I typed my "yes" response to Driesen. I had only two hours to leave work, pack, and catch a flight departing at 5:50 p.m. I was determined to testify in person. At that moment, I felt the presence of King Blue, who used his voice to appeal to leaders in our nation's capital on behalf of Blacks formerly enslaved by the Chickasaw Nation over a century ago. Despite my inner apprehensions and lack of trust in the process, I felt an overwhelming sense of honor. As the plane ascended in altitude, I imagined my ancestors smiling at me through the window as the sun began to set. I gazed up at the sky and fervently prayed that the sun would never set on our quest for justice. "I am because of them." *Ubuntu* is the African term for this connection. I exist because of them and they still exist because of me.

    It was especially important to me to use my voice at that moment. The Centennial of the Tulsa Race Massacre was around the corner. The event was being highly publicized and would bring Tulsa and its Race Massacre back to the nation's attention. For the Greenwood Historic

District, the Centennial was marked by a wonderful commemoration that honored survivors and descendants. The Black Wall Street Legacy Festival brought the spirit of unity and historic ownership back to Greenwood.

Bad news, however, was right around the corner. After some promising discoveries, the Oaklawn dig, as some called it, came to a sudden and screeching halt on June 25, 2021. For reasons never made clear, *the Oaklawn excavation was called off within 24 hours of finding a single male individual with gunshot wounds.* As soon as they found what they seemed to be looking for, they stopped! This decision was made without warning or consultation with the Oversight Committee. Nobody from City Hall has ever provided a compelling explanation for this suspicious cessation, and the City's representatives have provided contradictory information regarding who made the decision.[19]

Instead of answers, the City suddenly announced that it was going to rebury the previously exhumed remains back in the same hole from which they had been taken. A few representatives from the Mayor's office came to the Oversight Committee, asking for our "vote" concerning a reburial "ceremony." We unanimously rejected both the reburial itself and the proposed 'ceremony.' We

---

19 Randy Hopkins, "Echo of History,"note 26.

also registered our strong opposition to the "pause" in the investigation, as they now called it. Under the terms of the excavation plan, which the City asked the Committee to approve in early 2021, any reburial was to take place only *after* the Investigation was concluded. Under the terms of the contract that the City signed with the University of Oklahoma, the Oaklawn dig was set to last the entire summer and to exhume an area far beyond what had been accomplished to date. So, the dig hadn't been concluded; it had been suppressed.

Among my many objections was the decision, made over our heads, to rebury the remains in Oaklawn Cemetery. In joining the Oversight Committee, I told the city that if it was discovered that my DNA matched any of the remains, I would refuse to have them reburied in Oaklawn. A Tulsa man named Wyatt Tate Brady, a ringleader of the Oklahoma KKK, is buried there. The idea of reburying Jewish victims of the Holocaust in a Nazi or war criminal cemetery was unthinkable. How could the City of Tulsa proceed with such callousness and insensitivity?

Yet, proceed they did. On August 30, 2021, a largely white group of individuals said a brief prayer at the reburial site, and the City-owned earthmovers roared into action. Outside Oaklawn's locked iron fence, some Massacre victim descendants and others of the Greenwood community yelled in outrage, pain, and protest. If Mayor Bynum and the City of Tulsa had intended to create raw

4.3 Reburial in Oaklawn Cemetery.
Photo credit: City of Tulsa

images of racial division, they could have done no better job than what they caused to transpire on that day.

For me, the reburial was personal beyond my own family members. It exposed the wounds of generational trauma manifesting from collective memory. As a member of the Oversight Committee, I had the chance to see skeletal remains in the ground during the excavation. That experience was deeply spiritual for me. I knew that these souls were saying, "Thank you for finding us." And when we carried the remains to the lab, I spoke to the bones. And I asked the bones to speak to us. "Tell us why you are here." "Tell us your story." I experienced a profound connection with these specific remains that surpassed any rational comprehension. The final transported remains that I carried belonged to the male victim who had sustained the gunshot wound. I feel we received the evidence we needed to separate the Massacre victims from the Spanish Flu victims. The bones spoke loud and clear. That experience is the most remarkable part of this long journey to meet the needs of descendants. We need that connection. We need that communication. We need that affirmation that we are not doing this all for naught.

Since the sudden termination of the Oaklawn dig in June 2021, the Tulsa city authorities have continued to make a mockery of the Graves Investigation. Before the Centennial, all Oversight Committee meetings were open to the public, including many virtual meetings. All the meetings were recorded and promptly posted to the City's websites, where everyone could watch. Once the City was past the Centennial, however, the meetings have been "private" — the public is not allowed to attend or watch in real time. No recorded meetings have been posted since the Centennial. Since 2022, the City has refused to even record the meetings, which have been increasingly few in number. Those meetings are now lost to history. Yet, the City has long boasted of the Investigation's "transparency" and the important role of the Public Oversight Committee. That is falsehood and hypocrisy.

What the relevant City authorities fail to realize is how they have damaged themselves. Undoubtedly, yet another calculated betrayal has caused harm to members of the larger Greenwood community. But we are used to it! We're not surprised and it will not cause us to quit. The Mayor of Tulsa, in contrast, had a once-in-a-lifetime chance to be a true hero. To heal. To help free the future from the chains of the past. All that was required was that the promises he gave concerning the Investigation be kept. Yet, one-by-one, all the promises have been broken. There was no homicide investigation. The Oversight Committee was swept aside and under the rug. The Oaklawn dig was not finished when it could and should have been completed two years ago. There has been a complete lack of work at Newblock and elsewhere, not even testing. Instead of heroism, the City has instead chosen to channel the spirits of the unheroic past. Hopefully, future City leaders will do better.

In conclusion, I offer you my words of testimony that I gave to Congress in Washington, D. C. on May 19, 2021. I carried my sacred custodianship of both the recovered bones in Oaklawn and the still-unrecovered bones that may lie in other pieces of Greenwood's sacred ground now scattered around Tulsa. In that same vein, I honor the courageous survivors and advocates who testified on Capitol Hill before the Congressional Black Caucus on Tuesday, May 10, 2005, in Washington, D.C. Among them were survivor Wess Young, who at the time was 88 years of age, Dr. Olivia Hooker, 90, and Otis Granville Clark, who was 102. Among those advocating for the survivors were the Honorable Professor Charles Ogletree, and our beloved Eddie Faye Gates. May they always be remembered, along with the many others who joined them. I have dedicated nearly half of my life to the cause of reparatory justice. The journey is still ongoing. On May 19, 2021, I traveled to Washington, DC, where the last known surviving eyewitnesses of the Tulsa massacre were scheduled to testify. Two of the survivors were physically present, as was their attorney, Damario Solomon Simmons. Three descendants, including myself, State Representative Regina Goodwin, and Dr. Tiffany Crutcher, were present to testify before the Civil Rights and Civil Liberties Subcommittee of the US House of Representatives Judiciary Committee as well. Hughes Van Ellis, 100, Viola Ford Fletcher, 107, and Lessie Benningfield Randle, 106. After one hundred years, they were given the chance to convey their truth for the entire world to witness. I am grateful to have been able to follow in their footsteps. This is my own testimony:

Thank you, Mr. Chairman and esteemed body, My name is Chief Egunwale Amusan. I am the grandson of Raymond Beard, Sr., and the grandnephew of Matthew and Mary Beard, all of whom were survivors of the 1921 Tulsa Holocaust, massacre, or any other matching descriptor.

4.4 My testimony before Congress. This Still image is from the video coverage at the Hearing before the Subcommittee on the Constitution, Civil Rights, and Civil Liberties of the Committee onthe Judiciary. U.S. House of Representatives, Wednesday, May 19, 2021, Washington, D.C.

I was born and raised in Tulsa, Oklahoma. Today I speak on behalf of those whose remains were dumped carelessly in the Arkansas River by the truckloads; those remains that cracked the concrete from beneath the highway built over them; those remains dumped in mass graves, like the one I stood in October of 2020 during the mass grave investigation at Oaklawn Cemetery in Tulsa.

As a Member of the Mass Graves Oversight Committee, I stood in that trench with 12 coffins that we uncovered. I couldn't help but to be drawn to a smaller box, which appeared to be the size of a woman's hat box. It triggered the memory of something I had read in the Race Riot Commission report in 2001.

I rushed home to look at that document again, and it

stated that the remains in the trench were not embalmed, and the death certificates were not even signed by a medical examiner, a process undignified in every respect. The document stated that Tulsa County paid Stanley McCune Funeral Home to bury 16 bodies in the city cemetery. The report states that 4 of the 16 bodies placed in the mass grave were babies, and one was that of a stillborn baby.

When I returned, I looked again at the box in the trench. I walked away and wept for the soul of this child and the mother, who would never know the whereabouts of her child, lost both in the womb and in the earth.

Our family's journey to Greenwood actually started 139 years ago when my children's fourth great-grandfather named King Blue co-wrote a letter submitted to Congress and the House of Representatives, just as I am doing today. King Blue was a former slave of the Chickasaw tribal leader Benjamin Colbert. He and other tribal representatives presented a document in 1882 called the Memorial of the Chickasaw Freedmen.

The intent of this appeal was to encourage the enforcement of the 1866 treaty that obliges the tribe to carry out the third clause which states, "The monies given by the Federal Government to the tribe requires the tribe grant freed persons all the rights, privileges and immunities, including the right of suffrage." The Chickasaw Nation refused to honor the treaty. So, my relatives were nationless for 40 years, until 1902, when, through an Act of Congress, thousands of forgotten enslaved Africans were made citizens of the United States of America.

Around that time, my Freedmen ancestors and those of my spouse migrated to Tulsa's Greenwood district. Greenwood brought a new sense of self-determination and restored dignity, but one that would be short-lived. The dreamland of Tulsa became a nightmare. Over the course of just a few decades, my ancestors experienced enslavement, false freedom, Jim Crow, and a holocaust that would be hidden from the pages of history for 100 years.

Fast forward, it wasn't until 1997 that I became deeply aware of the Tulsa holocaust and its implications. However, I remained unaware of my family's involvement until my grandfather became a plaintiff in the reparation suit of 2003. I felt a full range of emotions and unanswered questions. Today, I regret that I asked too many questions because I was unaware of the trauma that I was invoking.

The long-term implications of the Tulsa Holocaust in urban renewal can physically be seen today. This is not a matter of past trauma; it is concurrent. It is concurrent trauma. The long-term implications, again, of this holocaust, can be seen physically today.

The plot to destroy the Black township of Greenwood was not a spontaneous Act caused by a rumor [about an attempted] assault in an elevator. It was premeditated as well as racially and politically motivated. Many who discover the story of Greenwood cannot fathom that such a place was built, nor can they believe that this type of terrorism happened on American soil, on domestic soil.

The violations of the 14th Amendment were not the result of a crazed mob. This was a city-sanctioned violation. The event resulted in the deprivation of life, liberty, and property without due process of law, as well as the failure to provide equal protection of the law.

Greenwood was a cultural, social, and economic incubator, an environment that provided apprenticeships and other high standards [for youth]. It was economic, political, and social stability. Most importantly, it provided a safe place to finally heal and detox individually and collectively from the effects of post-traumatic slave syndrome.

According to a 2019 story in *The Harvard Gazette*, the property damage in today's numbers were estimated to be as high as $200 million. The highest form of devastation was the mental suffering that resulted in high rates of PTSD and other forms of psychological morbidity, such as depression, anxiety, and homelessness.

Many of those who speak of Greenwood often reference the resilience of Greenwood's inhabitants because they rebuilt much of the district by 1925.

As remarkable as it is, only an estimated 40% of

those original inhabitants actually returned to Greenwood. My grandfather's eldest siblings were his caretakers. Both disappeared after the massacre, never to return. Their home and laundry business were burned to ashes. We later discovered that my Great Uncle Matthew Beard fled to Los Angeles, where he and his wife changed their first names to conceal their identity.

One cannot imagine the trauma of not knowing if a family member is dead or alive. Now, I understand why my grandfather always said, "No news is good news."

My grandfather would return to Greenwood in the 1940s to see it destroyed again in urban renewal. In 2003, my grandfather passed away a few months after becoming a plaintiff in the reparations' lawsuit filed by Johnnie Cochran and Charles Ogletree. According to the Supreme Court, this case would not be heard because the statute of limitations had run out.

Today, the same city responsible for the crimes of 1921 is leveraging the suffering of three living survivors in the name of tourism. When I look my oldest son in the eyes, I wonder if the charred baton of justice will burn in the palms of his hands, or will it be cleansed and cooled in the river of restitution?

Epilogue

In 2021, I was interviewed by Salima Koroma, the Emmy Award winning director of the documentary *Dreamland: The Burning of Black Wall Street*. She asked me to describe "Black Wall Street." I said that it was like Wakanda (the comic based fictional African Kingdom that was self-sustaining) and oil was vibranium (a metal in Wakanda that created kinetic energy). Black Wall Street and the entirety of Greenwood sat right in the middle of the Oil capital of the World.

Some believe that we romanticize and embellish the story of Greenwood. Efforts have even been made to minimize the number of wealthy residents in the Greenwood district. This book is not written or expressed through the optic of privilege, but through an optic of success, struggle, and survival. How does Greenwood appear through the eyes of a black Freedman who was not even a generation removed from Native American and White American slavery? There is no greater wealth than blackbody liberty and property ownership for one who was once enslaved. Wealth for the black Freedmen cannot be measured by the shallow vision of the entitled. Individual status was not the only determinant of wealth in Greenwood. A common focal point served as the measurement. An affluent household consists of multiple families and multiple income sources. When comparing the number of homes in Greenwood to the district's population, it is evident that there were many affluent households. A perspective oblivious to most who have tried to redefine and narrate the Black experience from the perspective of the hunter and not the Lion.

Over twenty years ago, a collective group of like-minded community members collaborated to form the Black Wall Street Memorial March. That same group evolved into what is now known as the Tulsa African Ancestral Society, also known as Egbe Egun Fe Wa. I function as its President. The African Ancestral Society was commissioned in Abeokuta, Nigeria by the High Chief Oluwo Fasesan Fagbenro Amusan of Ibara. These societies date back more than 400 years in West Africa. The African Ancestral Society's aim is to personally and collectively honor the memory of our ancestors. One of the first things that the Tulsa African Ancestral Society did to honor our ancestors was to take a stand against being written out of History.

The Black Wall Street Memorial March honors the pioneers, survivors, and descendants of Tulsa's Greenwood District (also known as Black Wall Street). This Memorial Day weekend march has been held on the sacred grounds of Greenwood for nearly three decades. At the request of the survivors, the Tulsa African Ancestral Society endeavors to ensure they are never forgotten. Our endeavors have included free lectures, scholarships for descendants, conferences, and ceremonies to honor the survivors, living and deceased.

It wasn't until around 2003 that I discovered my family's connection to the Massacre. Prior to this day, I was oblivious. I was Attorney Johnnie Cochran's security detail when he visited Tulsa for a press conference at the Greenwood Cultural Center with Harvard Law Professor Charles Ogletree and Civil Rights Activist Randall Robinson. As I scanned the crowd, I was shocked and excited to see my grandfather in the audience. I went over to greet him, and I asked "What brought you out today"? He replied, "Have a seat, son. I was in Tulsa during the riot. I'm a survivor." I was devastated to discover this about my grandfather. The world stopped turning for a minute. The weight of one century of silence and trauma caused by the massacre entered my own body with great heaviness. I had so many questions. I had more questions than I had the right to ask of my grandfather Raymond, because to ask him to tell his story was to ask him to revisit a childhood trauma. We didn't use the language of "trauma" at the time, but I instinctively knew I had to proceed with caution when we did speak. I have learned that when a story gets disrupted within families, the next generation bears the injury in their own way, compounding the harm. I know my family members had to flee for their lives. My great-grandmother, Eliza Gibbs, had been sick for some time; she was no longer able to care for my grandfather by the time he turned nine. Another of Raymond's sisters, Lorraine, took care of him, and they eventually settled in Kansas. Raymond was living in Independence when he registered for the draft for World War II.

The long silence carried in families and in the Greenwood community about the Massacre is no accident. Violence created this silence, and the internalization of that violence has allowed it to last for over 100 years. It is no accident that the *Tulsa Star* newspaper office was destroyed in the attack in 1921 or that highly articulate Tulsans like Smitherman and Stradford were targeted with arrest warrants, death threats, and warnings to never come back to Oklahoma. Generations have been haunted by the fear of retribution. Keeping silent has been a form of self-protection, and ethically prudent.

A few years back, I accompanied a National Public Radio reporter to the home of my Godparents Wess and Catherine Young, Wess was a child at the time of the attack. The reporter asked the usual question: "Why doesn't anyone talk about the Massacre?" Mrs. Young, as elegant and dignified a lady as you will ever meet, broke character. She sat back in her chair and said plainly, "Because they would kill us." The fear of reprisal still haunts Greenwood. Yet, keeping silent can also compound harm. I treat the injuries of the past very gingerly when it comes to community members and family.

I treat the injustices of the past without apology when it comes to the perpetrators and their protectors. I have called the entire city of Tulsa a mass grave, a site of collective and individual injury. Tulsa is undoubtedly the site where true heroes, and patriots stood strong in the face of thousands. Successfully they defended Greenwood's dignity on May 31st 1921. They are to its descendants what Leonidas and the 300 spartans were to the Greeks. They too were eventually overrun. Tulsa must also be a site of healing. Greenwood is also a site of wounding and loss. It is also a landmark of grand success and sacred remembrance . This is my life's work. I would dare venture to say that one day this will inspire one of the most remarkable films about one of the most remarkable places ever known — Ode to Greenwood!

Acknowledgements

I am indebted to Mary Parrish, Mable B. Little, B.C. Franklin, A.J. Smitherman, Dorothy Dewitty, Ron Wallace, and Eddie Faye Gates for their invaluable contribution of ancestral knowledge to this book. To my beloved parents Raymond Beard Jr. and Sarah Beard, you have my unending gratitude. Thank you for teaching me to honor my roots, and effectively employ my own words. Ifakemi Amusan, my beloved wife. Thank you for your tolerance and support throughout this arduous process. You are my crown's guardian. Massacre Survivor Wess Young. My adoptive grandfather whose words "never let them forget us" are etched into the pages of this book. Thank you, Tricia Woodgett, my amazing and brilliant friend. Thank you for proving to me what is possible when we tell our own story. Brother-in-law Sergeant First Class Charles Harding, a descendant of King Blue and family historian, thank you for sharing your extensive knowledge. Thank you to the triplets. Ogunbunmi Fagbenro, thank you for keeping me disciplined and on task. Osunbunmi Fagbenro thank you for your divine purpose driven prayers. Egunbunmi Fagbenro thank you for helping me visualize how big this really is. Representative Regina Goodwin, thank you for demonstrating why it is important to make people sit up when you enter a room. Dreisen Heath, I owe you a debt of gratitude for establishing the standard for flawless research. Your talent has left an enduring impression on the content of this book. Erna Brodber, Queen Mother, accomplished author, and community builder. Never will I forget kneeling before you as you instructed me, in a firm but kind manner, to write the histories of our people. Thank you, Councilwoman Vanessa Hall Harper for the creation of the mass graves oversight committee, and for demanding accountability for those interred in mass graves all over the City of Tulsa. Significant thanks to Kavin Ross, the torchlight bearer in the search for mass graves. Rest in peace my friend. Thank you, Don Ross and the Greenwood Cultural Center, for building and sustaining our house of historical memory on sacred ground. Heartfelt thanks to Milton Goodwin, James Goodwin, Leroy Thomas, and Greenwood Chamber president Ralph McIntosh for their sacrifice and efforts to preserve the tangible assets in the 100 block of North Greenwood in the late 1970's. We are indebted to you for what exists today. Thank you, Dr. Tiffany Crutcher, Justice for Greenwood, and Tulsa Community Remembrance Coalition, for consistently demanding restitution, respect and repair.

Thanks to the "Who We Are Project" creators Jeffrey Robinson, Andrea Crabtree, Sarah, and Emily Kunstler. This book was inspired by your brilliant, and effective teaching approach. Huge acknowledgement to Whitney Chapman, Traci Chapman and the Center for Public Secrets for showing Tulsa what it means to be a co-conspirator in the fight for truth and justice. Thanks to the Center there are voices, and stories that will never be forgotten, and truths that will no longer remain hidden. Thank you to my amazing research collaborators, historical scholars Randy Hopkins and Patricia Schechter.

Thank you both for historically and academically supporting and understanding the necessity for this book. Thank you, Lee Roy Chapman, for passing on the skill that comes with being a history recovery specialist. Rest eternal! Big thanks to the Actor, Author Tom Hanks, who took The Real Black Wall Street Tour and reminded Tulsa that the omission of this history robs America of the enrichment of who we are as Americans.

Huge thanks to Well-Told's Stuart Hetherwood and

Ryan McGahan for being professional co-conspirators in the development and design of this important work. Joseph Rushmore, thank you for always being where the ancestors placed you to capture images that are sacred.

Thank you to everyone who has had the courage to educate, fight, and preserve the legacy of the Greenwood Historic District. You know who you are. You are not forgotten. My deepest respect is extended to Lessie Benningfield Randle, Viola Ford Fletcher, and our cherished predecessor, Hughes Van Ellis, who departed at the extraordinary age of 102 on October 9, 2023.

Although their number has decreased, the known surviving victims of the Tulsa Massacre have magnified in spirit. Your courage, resilience, and testament all serve to motivate me. Your story is having an impact across the globe. You have my gratitude, admiration, and regard.

I will close this writing with just two more acknowledgments. The first goes to the man who has fought by my side and on the side of justice for more than 20 years in Tulsa. Together, and also in different and distinct ways, we have amplified justice activism and educational outreach in Tulsa. Attorney Damario Solomon-Simmons needs no introduction. He has been a brilliant and devoted advocate in the legal fight for reparations for the survivors and descendants of the Tulsa Race Massacre. He has also been a leading voice for the civil rights of the

A.1 Love is the Resistance A.2. with Dr. Cornel West. Photos courtesy of author.

descendants of the Freedmen in Oklahoma, specifically those connected to the Creek Nation. He founded the Justice for Greenwood Foundation to help advance the fight. I proudly wear my purple JFG shirt on occasion when I conduct my Real Black Wall Street Tours. Damario, you are my brother in this struggle. May the brilliance and knowledge of the late Professor Charles Ogletree and the late Attorney Johnnie Cochran carry you forward on this battle toward repair and restitution.

On the tour, I also wear a hoodie with the words "Love is the Resistance" printed across the front. There is a story behind this sweatshirt. It connects to another brilliant son of Tulsa, Dr. Cornel West. Dr. West is an internationally known scholar, theologian, and public intellectual who has written 20 books and even cut a rap CD! He taught at Harvard University for many years and has appeared on TV, movies, and in a podcast called "The Tightrope" (one of his books is titled Hope on a Tightrope).

In 2017, I attended the Zarrow mental health symposium with the theme "Challenging Injustice and Discrimination" in Tulsa. Dr. West gave a rousing and unforgettable keynote address at this meeting. There were many fans and well-wishers who wanted to shake his hand or get an autograph. I waited and waited until the people thinned out. I needed to connect with this man whose message about love had so moved me. In the brief moments that I spent with Dr. West, he said something that reshaped my life's purpose. He proclaimed, "If the kingdom of God is within you then everywhere you go you leave a little bit of heaven behind. You're gonna leave the world better than you found it. You're gonna leave the world with a little more love, and justice is what that love looks like in public."

Bibliography

Primary Sources

Archives
Tulsa, Oklahoma
Tulsa Historical Society
 Red Cross Reports (1921)

Wilmington, NC
University of North Carolina, Wilmington
 1898 Foundation Papers

Online repositories
Ancestry.com (census and related materials)

History Vault: The NAACP Papers

National Archives of the United States, Washington, D.C.
RG 75 — Records of the Bureau of Indian Affairs

Newspapers and Publications
The Buffalo & Erie Public Library (Grosvenor Room)

The *Empire Star* Newspaper, 1960

Library of Congress
Chronicling America: Historic American Newspapers
https://chroniclingamerica.loc.gov/

Tulsa Daily World, *Tulsa Star*, etc.

Memoir, Autobiography, Oral Testimony
Continuing Injustice: The Centennial of the Tulsa-Greenwood Race Massacre. Hearing before the Subcommittee on the Constitution, Civil Rights, and Civil Liberties of the Committee on the Judiciary. U.S. House of Representatives 117th Congress, first session. Wednesday, May 19, 2021. https://www.congress.gov/event/117th-congress/house-event/LC69006/text?s=1&r=99

Du Bois, W. E. B. *Dusk of Dawn: An Essay toward an Autobiography of a Race Concept.* New York: Harcourt, Brace and Co., 1940.

Ellison, Ralph. *Going to the Territory.* New York: Random House, 1986.

Franklin, Buck Colbert. *My Life and an Era: The Autobiography of Buck Colbert Franklin.* Baton Rouge: Louisiana State University Press, 1997.

Gates, Eddie Faye. *Riot on Greenwood: The Total Destruction of Black Wall Street.* Austin, Tex: Eakin Press, 2003.

Tulsa-Greenwood Race Riot Claims Accountability Act of 2007: Hearing before the Subcommittee on the Constitution, Civil Rights, and Civil Liberties of the Committee on the Judiciary, House of Representatives, One Hundred Tenth Congress, First Session, on H.R. 1995, April 24, 2007. Washington: U.S. G.P.O, 2007.

Wallace, Michele. *Invisibility Blues: From Pop to Theory.* New York: Verso, 1990.

Select Secondary Sources

Aiyetoro, Adjoa. "Achieving Reparations While Respecting Our Differences: A Model for Black Reparations." *Howard Law Journal* 63, no. 3 (2020): 329–48.

Andrews, Thomas F. "Freedmen in Indian Territory: A Post-Civil War Dilemma." *The Journal of the West* 4, no. 3 (July 1965): 367–76.

Brooks, James. *Confounding the Color Line: The Indian-Black Experience in North America.* Lincoln: University of Nebraska Press, 2002.

Brophy, Alfred L. *Reconstructing the Dreamland the Tulsa Riot of 1921: Race, Reparations, and Reconciliation.* New York: Oxford University Press, 2002.

Brundage, W. Fitzhugh. *Lynching in the New South: Georgia and Virginia, 1880-1930.* Urbana: University of Illinois Press, 1993.

Cain, Ellen. "'The Golden Days': Taylor and Mary Ealy, Citizenship, and the Freedmen of Chickasaw Indian Territory, 1874-77." *Chronicles of Oklahoma* 92, no. 1 (Spring 2014): 54–77.

Clegg, Claude A. *The Price of Liberty: African Americans and the Making of Liberia.* Chapel Hill: University of North Carolina Press, 2004.

Clegg, Claude A. *Troubled Ground: A Tale of Murder, Lynching, and Reckoning in the New South.* Champagne: University of Illinois Press, 2010.

Danielson, Chris. "'Lily White and Hard Right": The Mississippi Republican Party and Black Voting, 1965-1980." *The Journal of Southern History* 75, no. 1 (2009): 83-118.

Darcy, R. "Did Oklahoma African Americans Vote Between 1910 and 1943?" *Chronicles of Oklahoma* 93, no. 1 (Spring 2015): 72-98.

Ellsworth, Scott. *Death in a Promised Land: The Tulsa Race Riot of 1921.* Baton Rouge: Louisiana State University Press, 1982.

Emberton, Carole. *Beyond Redemption: Race, Violence, and the American South after the Civil War.* Chicago; The University of Chicago Press, 2013.

Feimster, Crystal Nicole. *Southern Horrors: Women and the Politics of Rape and Lynching.* Cambridge, Mass: Harvard University Press, 2009.

Feldman, Glenn. *The Irony of the Solid South: Democrats, Republicans, and Race, 1865-1944.* Tuscaloosa: The University of Alabama Press, 2013.

Franklin, Jimmie Lewis. *Born Sober: Prohibition in Oklahoma, 1907-1959.* Norman: University of Oklahoma Press, 1971.

Gayle, Caleb. *We Refuse to Forget: A True Story of Black Creeks, American Identity, and Power.* New York: Riverhead Books, 2022.

Gritter, Elizabeth. *River of Hope: Black Politics and the Memphis Freedom Movement, 1865-1954.* Lexington, Kentucky: University Press of Kentucky, 2014.

Hendricks, Anthony. "Guinn v. U.S.: State's Rights and the 15th Amendment." *Oklahoma Bar Association* (blog), May 4, 2021. https://www.okbar.org/barjournal/may-2021/hendricks-2021/.

Hine, Darlene Clark, and Steven F. Lawson. *Black Victory: The Rise and Fall of the White Primary in Texas.* Columbia: University of Missouri Press, 2003.

Hirsch, James S. *Riot and Remembrance: The Tulsa Race War and Its Legacy*. Boston: Houghton Mifflin Company, 2002.

Hopkins, Randy. "Mask of Atonement: Mark of the Hun." *The Tulsa Race Massacre: Teaching and Learning Resources*, January 1, 2021. https://pdxscholar.library.pdx.edu/tulsa/2.

———. "The Plot to Kill 'Diamond Dick' Rowland and the Tulsa Race Massacre." The Chronicles of Oklahoma 99, no. 1 (Spring 2021): 4-49.

———. "The Notorious Sarah Page," https://www.centerforpublicsecrets.org/post/the-notorious-sarah-page

———. "Echo of History: The City of Tulsa's Mass Graves Debacle," https://www.centerforpublicsecrets.org/post/echo-of-history-the-city-of-tulsa-s-mass-graves-debacle.

Johnson, Hannibal B., *Black Wall Street: From Riot to Renaissance in Tulsa's Historic Greenwood District*. Eakin Press, 2007.

Krehbiel, Randy. *Tulsa 1921: Reporting a Massacre*. Norman, OK: University of Oklahoma Press, 2019.

Kousser, J. Morgan. *The Shaping of Southern Politics: Suffrage Restriction and the Establishment of the One-Party South, 1880-1910*. New Haven: Yale University Press, 1974.

Littlefield, Daniel F. *The Chickasaw Freedmen: A People without a Country*. Westport, Conn: Greenwood Press, 1980.

Madigan, Tim. *The Burning: Massacre, Destruction, and the Tulsa Race Riot of 1921*. New York: Thomas Dunne Books/St. Martin's Press, 2001.

Magliulo, Myrna. "Andrew J. Smitherman: A Pioneer of the African American Press, 1909-1961." *Afro-Americans in New York Life and History* 34, no. 2 (2010): 119-53.

Mickey, Robert. *Paths out of Dixie: The Democratization of Authoritarian Enclaves in America's Deep South, 1944-1972*. Princeton, New Jersey: Princeton University Press, 2015.

Nevergold, Barbara A Seals. "A. J. Smitherman: Pen Warrior." *Chronicles of Oklahoma* 89, no. 3 (2011): 288-311.

Ogletree, Jr, and Austin Sarat, eds. *When Law Fails: Making Sense of Miscarriages of Justice.* New York: NYU Press, 2009.

Oklahoma Commission to Study the Tulsa Race Riot of 1921. "Tulsa Race Riot: A Report by the Oklahoma Commission To Study the Tulsa Race Riot of 1921." Copy in Oklahoma Historical Society.

Oks, David. "The Election of 1916, 'Negrowumpism,' and the Black Defection from the Republican Party." *The Journal of the Gilded Age and Progressive Era* 20, no. 4 (2021): 523-47.

Painter, Nell Irvin. *Exodusters: Black Migration to Kansas after Reconstruction.* New York: Knopf, 1977.

Perman, Michael. *Struggle for Mastery: Disfranchisement in the South, 1888-1908.* Chapel Hill: University of North Carolina Press, 2001.

Riser, R. Volney. *Defying Disfranchisement: Black Voting Rights Activism in the Jim Crow South, 1890-1908.* Baton Rouge: LSU Press, 2010.

Robinson, Stephen. "'To Think, Act, Vote, and Speak for Ourselves': Black Democrats and Black 'Agency' in the American South after Reconstruction." *Journal of Social History* 48, no. 2 (2014): 363-82.

Scales, James R. *Oklahoma Politics: A History.* Norman, Okla: University of Oklahoma Press, 1982.

Tyler-McGraw, Marie. *An African Republic: Black & White Virginians in the Making of Liberia.* Chapel Hill: University of North Carolina Press, 2007.

Wallace, Ron. *Black Wall Street.* Tulsa: Black Wall Street Publishing & Dularon Entertainment, 1992.

West, Cornel. *Hope on a Tightrope: Words & Wisdom.* Carlsbad, Calif: Smiley Books, 2008.

Raymond Beard Sr. (Grandpa)
Your Bones Have Been Recovered